The Apostles' Creed

The Apostles' Creed

A User's Guide

Marshall D. Johnson

Augsburg Books

MINNEAPOLIS

Cover image: Photo © Stockbyte / Getty Images. Used by permission.
Cover design: Mudville Design
Interior design: PerfecType, Nashville, TN

Library of Congress Cataloging-in-Publication Data

Johnson, Marshall D.
    The Apostles' Creed : a user's guide / Marshall D. Johnson.
        p. cm.
    Includes bibliographical references (p. 101) and index.
    ISBN 978-0-8066-8051-4 (alk. paper)
    1. Apostles' Creed. I. Title.

    BT993.3.J64 2008
    238'.11--dc22
                                            2008028041

The paper used in this publication meets the minimum requirements of American National Standard for Information Sciences—Permanence of Paper for Printed Library Materials, ANSI Z329.48-1984.

Manufactured in the U.S.A.

12   11   10   09   08   1   2   3   4   5   6   7   8   9   10

Contents

The Apostles' Creed

I believe in God, the Father almighty,
    creator of heaven and earth.

I believe in Jesus Christ, God's only Son, our Lord,
    who was conceived by the Holy Spirit,
    born of the virgin Mary,
    suffered under Pontius Pilate,
    was crucified, died, and was buried;
    he descended to the dead.
    On the third day he rose again;
    he ascended into heaven;
    he is seated at the right hand of the Father;
    and he will come to judge the living and the dead.

I believe in the Holy Spirit,
    the holy catholic church,
    the communion of saints,
    the forgiveness of sins,
    the resurrection of the body,
    and the life everlasting. Amen.

A Note to the Reader

Christians over the past twenty centuries have often labored to express their faith in words. As we repeat an ancient creed during our worship services, however, the specific situations in the real lives of human beings from which these statements arose are sometimes only vaguely sensed. Understanding the original purpose of our creeds can do much to heighten our appreciation of these venerable words and, at the same time, to bring clarity to our understanding of what we believe.

Many persons have written explanations of the Apostles' Creed from various perspectives and for diverse groups of readers. This book is distinctive in three main ways: (1) it deals with the gap in the creed between Jesus' birth and his death, (2) it emphasizes how the resurrection of Jesus is the pattern for much of the Christian hope, and (3) it explains in detail how the creed originated in opposition to Christian sects known as Gnostics.

I offer this book as a resource both for individuals and for group study in the hope that it will be useful for lifelong church members who seek a refresher in some of the central affirmations of the faith as well as for those preparing for church membership.

1

Why Creeds?

"I BELIEVE. . . ." What does it mean to speak these words in our time? From all corners we hear competing truth claims. People of various faiths or of no discernible faith live side by side. Religious fervor causes division in political elections. It seems clear that Western societies in the twenty-first century have entered the "postmodern" epoch, with its assumptions that truth claims are relative, making it necessary to live with tolerance and ambiguity.

A creed is a statement of what we believe or trust. Your *actual* faith is what you entrust your life to—the direction in which your personal being is oriented. But if spirituality were entirely a private matter, perhaps creeds would not be necessary; each person could have his or her distinctive beliefs and practices without sharing them with others. Without clearly understood written formulations and affirmations, however, the Christian church could only with great difficulty sustain itself over the generations, and it would struggle to describe what holds it together as a community, the "communion of saints." The creeds of the church, while spoken by individuals, are always community statements—faith statements of the fellowship of believers.

The Function of Creeds

Christian creeds, whether from ancient times or today, function in three basic ways. (1) In our time of competing voices and confusing claims, our creeds identify specific affirmations that our community holds to be essential to its being. They define who we are and what undergirds our lives as individuals and as a group. (2) They draw a line between beliefs that can be accepted within the community and those that must be rejected. This is often done without the use of negating language. For example, some ancient Christian groups contended that Jesus revealed a different god from the one who created the heavens and the earth. The Apostles' Creed explicitly rejects this idea, not with a condemning statement, but by the positive assertion that God the Creator is the Father of Jesus. (3) Christians have always used creeds as a manual of instruction for new members—or for young people who are about to take on adult roles in the church.

What is involved when we say, "I believe. . ."? According to traditional Christian teaching, faith—believing—has three components: knowledge, assent, and trust. First comes *knowledge* of what is to be believed; then we give *assent* to these truths; and finally we put our personal *trust* in the object of our faith. The difference between assent and trust is often expressed by reference to James 2:19, which asserts that even the demons know and believe that God is one. The demons have the first two components of faith, knowledge and assent, but they by definition lack the third, *trust* in God's goodness and saving power. When we speak the words of the Apostles' Creed with fellow worshipers, we publicly declare our knowledge of and assent to Christian teachings. But trust in God the Father, his only Son, and the Holy Spirit is a personal and subjective matter for each individual in the community of faith.

No creed can adequately contain the whole range of Christian beliefs. The ancient creeds all reflect internal crises within the Christian movement, when conflicting ideas and practices threatened permanent divisions among the believers. Creeds are time-conditioned responses to specific and real conflict situations. We therefore misuse them when we take them to be a complete summary of what we are to believe or how we are to live. Have you ever noticed the most curious fact that the Apostles' Creed says nothing at all about the preaching and healing ministry of Jesus—or anything else that occurred between his birth and his suffering and death? As I note in the following chapters, the Apostles' Creed was formulated to deal with teachings about God and Jesus that most early church leaders found to be intolerable. Similarly, the Nicene Creed was originally composed in 325 A.D. to exclude the belief of some Egyptian Christians that Jesus was neither fully human nor fully divine, but something in between. Our ancient creeds are selective in their content. The affirmations are determined by—and are reactions to—specific conflicts in the early church.

Early Creeds

There are creedal statements already in the New Testament. The oldest and briefest may be the simple utterance in 1 Corinthians

12:3, "Jesus is Lord." When we realize that the Roman Empire in the first century was replete with "lords" and authorities, we can appreciate what a highly charged and potentially dangerous confession this was.

In addition, the following passages probably contain remnants of other early creeds:

- "[H]is Son . . . was descended from David according to the flesh and was declared to be Son of God with power according to the spirit of holiness by resurrection from the dead, Jesus Christ our Lord" (Romans 1:3–4).

Paul here seems to cite a formulation from his predecessors, one that stresses the humanity ("according to the flesh") and the divinity ("Son of God") of Jesus. It is striking, however, that Jesus' divine sonship is here dated to his resurrection rather than his birth or his preexistence.

- "Christ Jesus. . .
  though he was in the form of God,
      did not regard equality with God
      as something to be exploited,
  but emptied himself,
      taking the form of a slave,
      being born in human likeness.
  And being found in human form,
      he humbled himself
      and became obedient to the point of death—
      even death on a cross.
  Therefore God also highly exalted him
      and gave him the name
      that is above every name,
  so that at the name of Jesus

> every knee should bend,
>> in heaven and on earth and under the earth,
> and every tongue should confess
>> that Jesus Christ is Lord,
>>> to the glory of God the Father." (Philippians 2:5–11)

Many readers refer to this passage as a "Christ hymn," and most translations arrange it in the form of poetic lines. Differing from Romans 1:3–4, this hymn assigns divine glory to the preexistent Christ, who subjects himself to "human likeness" and an ignominious death. The beginnings of the doctrine of the incarnation (enfleshment) can be seen here. The pattern is glory→humiliation→glory.

- "He [Jesus] is the image of the invisible God, the first-born of all creation; for in him all things in heaven and on earth were created, things visible and invisible, whether thrones or dominions or rulers or powers—all things have been created through him and for him. He himself is before all things, and in him all things hold together. He is the head of the body, the church; he is the beginning, the firstborn from the dead, so that he might come to have first place in everything. For in him all the fullness of God was pleased to dwell, and through him God was pleased to reconcile to himself all things, whether on earth or in heaven, by making peace through the blood of his cross." (Colossians 1:15–20).

This hymn assigns to Christ preeminent status in the universe. Although many readers have found Greek influences here, it is more likely the result of scribal reflection on the first words of the Hebrew Bible: *bᵉ-reshith bara' elohim* (usually translated, "in the beginning God created. . ."). The Hebrew preposition *b^e* means "in," "through," or "by means of," and *reshith* or *rosh* means "head," "beginning." This Christ hymn identifies the pre-existent Christ with *reshith* or *rosh*, leading to the thought that creation took place "through" Christ, "the head. . .the beginning . . .the firstborn."

- "He [Jesus] was revealed in flesh,
    vindicated in spirit,
    seen by angels,
  proclaimed among Gentiles,
    believed in throughout the world,
    taken up in glory." (1 Timothy 3:16)

The Origin of the Apostles' Creed

A fanciful legend about the origin of the Apostles' Creed goes back to about 400 A.D. It tells how, on the day of Pentecost, after the apostles were enabled to speak in various tongues, God commanded them to preach in all the countries where those languages were spoken. Before leaving Jerusalem, the apostles came to a consensus on what they were to preach in those different cultures. Each of the Twelve contributed one statement; the resulting "apostles' creed" was to be the basis of their instruction of converts.

Historically speaking, we know today that a shorter form of the Apostles' Creed can be traced back to as early as 200 A.D., when the church at Rome had a three-part creed used as a confession of faith by persons about to be baptized. According to the theologian Hippolytus of Rome (approximately 170–236 A.D.) in his treatise *The Apostolic Tradition* 21.12ff., this creed was arranged as a series of three questions, and it read thus:

Do you believe in God the Father almighty?

Do you believe in Jesus Christ the Son of God, who was born of the Holy Spirit and the Virgin Mary, who was crucified under Pontius Pilate, died, and rose the third day living from the dead, and ascended into heaven, and sat down at the right hand of the Father, and will come to judge the living and the dead?

Do you believe in the Holy Spirit, and the holy church, and the resurrection of the flesh?

This "Old Roman Creed" apparently did not include the words "creator of heaven and earth" (although that belief was clearly presupposed), "only" [Son], "our Lord," "conceived," "suffered," "buried," "descended into hell," "catholic," "communion of saints," "forgiveness of sins," and "life everlasting." These words were added at some point between the fourth and the sixth centuries. The Old Roman Creed, however, is certainly the ancestor of the Apostles' Creed that we confess yet today.

The oldest form of our creed was originally formulated to exclude sectarian believers now known as "Gnostics" (*gnosis* in Greek means "knowledge"). This movement, composed of widely varying mystical, religious-philosophical groups in the first three centuries, is difficult to define or even to describe. In general, however, it was a religion of personal redemption based on a sharp dualism between spirit and matter. Gnostics were convinced that this world was evil—for some, it was hell—and certainly not the creation of the supreme God, who in Gnosticism remained completely unknowable apart from revelation. This world, they held, arose either from the actions of a lesser or hostile deity (for some, this was the God of the Old Testament) or from downward emanations (variously called "archons," "authorities," "heavens," "planets," and so on) from the realm of pure spirit. According to Gnostics, therefore, the God of the Old Testament was not the God revealed by Jesus—the previously unknown, fully transcendent Supreme Being. Thus they separated creation from redemption. Their dualism of spirit and matter, moreover, led them generally to make a sharp distinction between the human "Jesus" and the divine "Christ," "Logos," or "Son." Some Gnostics held that the divine Son or Logos entered into the human body of Jesus at his baptism, abandoning the body before the crucifixion. Others thought that the body of Jesus was a phantom, merely seeming to be real. Regarding human beings, they taught that everyone has a body and a soul, and a few have also the "divine spark," a remnant of the spiritual realm. Redemption occurs when this spark is kindled by knowledge (*gnosis*) of the origin of the world and especially of the supreme God. Salvation comes by mystical ascent of the individual to the spiritual reality and ultimate union with the "fullness" of that realm. Many Gnostics included belief in a redeemer figure whose function it was to reveal—to teach—and most certainly not to die a humiliating death and rise again. Gnostic contempt for this world resulted in moral extremes. Some were ascetic and world-denying while others allowed libertinism on the grounds that the flesh counts for nothing.

After the Old Roman Creed gained general acceptance, with its insistence on the oneness of the almighty God, the Creator and the Father of Jesus, and the reality of Jesus' birth, suffering, death, and resurrection, no member of a Gnostic cult could enjoy normal fellowship with the churches that accepted the creed. (I say more about this in the chapters below.)

The Three Articles

The three articles in the Apostles' Creed correspond to the three "persons" of the Trinity—Father, Son, and Spirit. The roots of the teaching about the Trinity go back to New Testament expressions like Matthew 28:19, "Go therefore and make disciples of all nations, baptizing them in the name of the *Father* and of the *Son* and of the *Holy Spirit.*" Romans 1:1–4 mentions "the gospel of *God*," "his *Son*," and "the *spirit* of holiness." Galatians 4:6 also mentions the three: "*God* has sent the *Spirit* of his *Son* into our hearts." And 2 Corinthians 13:13 links the three in a classic benediction: "The grace of the *Lord Jesus Christ*, the love of *God*, and the communion of the *Holy Spirit* be with all of you" (emphasis mine). The doctrine of the Trinity goes beyond these biblical statements and asserts that God is one in "substance" or "being" and three in "person." There are not three gods but rather three persons within the one Godhead.

The doctrine of the Trinity was initially developed by Christians at the Council of Nicea in 325 A.D., because they wanted to find a way to express their faith in Jesus without making him a second god or denying his status as the unique Son of God. Before that time there were several contrary opinions on the matter. Some thought that Jesus was adopted by God into a form of divinity. Others argued that God *was* Jesus and therefore one could say that the Father suffered and died on the cross. The matter came to a head in about 318 A.D. when Arius, a respected and aged priest in Alexandria, Egypt, taught that the divine aspect of Christ—the *Logos*—was not eternal but rather the first creation of God, created out of nothing. In the birth of Jesus this Logos entered a human body, fulfilling the functions of the mind or "soul" in other human beings. This made Jesus neither fully

God nor fully human but something in between. The Council of Nicea, after considerable discussion, declared that the Logos is "begotten, not made, of one Being with the Father." The Greek word for "one Being" is *homoousios*, "same essence," "same being," or "same substance."

The Old Roman Creed, the precursor of the Apostles' Creed, antedates the technical discussion that took place at Nicea in 325 A.D. Along with the Nicene Creed and the Athanasian Creed, it is one of the "three ecumenical creeds." In the Western churches today—both Protestant and Roman Catholic—the Apostles' Creed is the most widely used of all of Christendom's confessions of faith.

In our contemporary society, marked by mobility and diversity, the Apostles' Creed functions to create and maintain community among Christian believers over wide areas of the Western world. Although this creed says nothing about Christian *life*—how we are to live in this world—and although it does not tell us how we are to understand its individual assertions, it is a unifying force in a confusing time. It is, as theologians have long insisted, a "rule of faith" that has provided continuity from generations past into our own time.

2

I Believe in God, the Father Almighty, Creator of Heaven and Earth

ATHEISM WAS RARE in biblical times, and the atheist was considered both odd and foolish. Psalm 14:1 (also 53:1) is typical: "Fools say in their hearts, 'There is no God.'" If theoretical atheism is hardly to be found in the Bible, a kind of practical atheism is documented in both Testaments. That is to say, evildoers thought that God was removed from human affairs and would therefore not punish them. "In the pride of their countenance the wicked say, 'God will not seek it out'; all their thoughts are, 'There is no God'" (Psalm 10:4; also 73:11). A similar thought occurs in Jesus' parable of the rich man who was poor in relation to God (Luke 12:16–21). In biblical times, therefore, there was no need for "proofs" of God's existence, even though Paul in Romans 1:19–20 argues that the Gentiles have deliberately turned away from the worship of God, whose "eternal power and divine nature . . . have been understood and seen through the things he has made."

In contrast to the Bible, ancient Greek philosophers and medieval Christian theologians made strenuous efforts to prove God's existence by rational argument. Some suggested that there cannot be an endless chain of cause and effect in the universe; there must be a "First Cause" or a "Prime Mover," which we can call God. Others, in ways reminiscent of those in our time who hold to "intelligent design," argued that the natural world contains abundant evidence of planning and design in inanimate objects. How else can we explain the predictable movement of heavenly bodies or the predictable growth of plants from seeds? Still others used the "moral argument": the universal, innate human sense of duty and "oughtness" or conscience presupposes God's existence. And one medieval thinker, Anselm of Canterbury (1033–1109), believed that he could demonstrate God's existence from isolated human reflection:

> We can conceive in our minds the idea of something than which nothing can be greater. But if God does not exist, then anything that in fact does exist would be greater than God, for existence is greater than non-existence, and our conception of that than which nothing can be greater would be impossible.

The value of such arguments consists more in the assurance and comfort they provide to those who already believe than as incontrovertible demonstrations of God. Each of the arguments has weaknesses, and it would be difficult to identify anyone who came to faith by means of such speculations. There is a world of difference between believing and knowing. To *believe* in God means that we cannot *know* God in the way we know algebra or biology. We cannot prove the reality of God to someone who chooses not to believe, even though we might have sensed God's presence in our lives and found traces of God's work in the wonders of nature.

There is a problem in all such reflections more basic than the obvious gap between words and reality. To say that God "exists" leaves the impression that God is one being or object among a vast number of beings or objects. We know, however, that God is more than one being among others. God is the "ground of all being," the foundation of all that lives, the spiritual reality that permeates and underlies the very universe. That being the case, God, in the final analysis, is—quite literally—ineffable, beyond human words, transcending human imagination.

God as Almighty

The otherness and holiness of God are suggested by the word "almighty" in the First Article of the creed. We confess our faith and trust in "God the Father almighty." Medieval theologians tried to express the concept of God's transcendence by the use of "omni-" words: God is omniscient (all-knowing), omnipresent (ubiquitous), and omnipotent (all-powerful). Such thoughts have biblical precedent. Among ancient peoples who had national deities and tribal gods, ancient Israelites increasingly came to recognize Yahweh as the Lord of the universe: "The earth is the LORD's and all that is in it, the world, and those who live in it" (Psalm 24:1). "Dominion belongs to the LORD; and he rules over the nations" (Psalm 22:28). The oneness and power of God are most explicitly articulated in Isaiah 40–55, as, for example, Isaiah 40:22–23: "It is he who sits above the circle of the earth . . . who stretches out the heavens like a curtain . . . who brings princes to naught, and makes the rulers of the earth as nothing"; and 45:5, 7: "I am the LORD, and there is no other. . . . I form light and create darkness, I make weal and create woe; I the LORD do all these things." According to the Psalms and Isaiah, the power of God is evidenced most clearly in the acts of creation.

God the Creator

The Bible—poetically and metaphorically—asserts that God created the "heavens and the earth" by speech. "By the word of the LORD the heavens were made, and all their host by the breath of his mouth" (Psalm 33:6). This thought harks back to the repeated statement in Genesis 1, "And God *said*, 'Let there be. . . .'" God speaks, and it is so. (The impossibility of expressing such thoughts in scientific language is glaringly obvious.) The psalmist, in wonderful turns of phrase, adds that the heavens echo the creating speech of God, telling of God's glory (Psalm 19:1–2).

We cannot learn much from the Bible about *how* God created. But it is striking that in Genesis 1 creation consists of the bringing of increasing order out of primordial chaos. In a world of watery chaos and total darkness, God floods the scene with light, separates the heavens from the earth, separates the waters from the dry land on the earth, fills the waters and the dry land with living creatures, and ultimately calls forth human life—and the cause of all of this is God's speech.

For the past 150 years, the question of creation has been sidetracked and convoluted by one inflammatory word: *evolution*. Charles Darwin's argument in *The Origin of the Species* (1859) was twofold: (1) The species of plants and animals are not fixed and immutable from the hand of the Creator. Over unimaginably long periods of time, mutations occur in certain individuals; if these mutations are beneficial, they will ensure survival. Eventually such mutations will cause the formation of a new, usually more complex species. All species evolved from a few—or perhaps one—species. (2) This whole process is governed by a simple law, namely, natural selection. Those individuals and species best adapted to their environment survive, and the others become extinct. Many Christians reacted negatively and vehemently to such thoughts, mainly for two reasons. First, the theory seemingly reduced the role of the Creator to a minimum and excluded the idea of "creation out of nothing." Second, it minimized the boundary between human beings and other animals.

Darwin had predecessors, and his many successors have refined and honed his theory, finding compelling evidence in the discovery of ancient fossils and humanlike remains. Evolution is now much more than a hypothesis; it is a strong theory. Although in the early twenty-first century some persons still struggle mightily to marginalize this theory, they have not succeeded, and most Christians continue to see in Darwin's theory fresh evidence of God's method in creation. It should be obvious that Genesis speaks of the ultimate *cause* and origin of creation, while evolutionary theory speaks of the *way* it took place. The future coexistence of evolutionary theory and Christian belief seems certain. It is abundantly clear that a Christian can hold to evolutionary theories; an evolutionist can be a Christian.

God as Father

The First Article emphasizes the manifestation of God's mighty power in the acts of creation. But this is tempered in a surprising way by the use of a family metaphor: God is "Father."

Jesus, in his prayers, addressed God as *Abba* (the familiar Aramaic form of "Father," Mark 14:36). The apostle Paul confirms that the early Christians also addressed God as *Abba*, which he thought was made possible by the infusion of God's Spirit or the spirit of Jesus into the hearts of believers. The Holy Spirit is "bearing witness with our spirit that we are children of God" (Romans 8:15–16), and "God has sent the spirit of his Son into our hearts, crying, 'Abba! Father'" (Galatians 4:6). Moreover, God is referred to by almost all New Testament writers as *pater*, the Greek translation of Abba (*pater* occurs some 175 times in the New Testament).

Addressing God as Father antedates the New Testament. (1) God is specifically referred to as Father in the Old Testament, although only fourteen times. The poet confesses, "You, O Lord, are our father, our Redeemer from of old is your name" (Isaiah 63:16; see also 64:8). (2) Many personal names in the Old Testament include the Hebrew syllable *ab* (father) as referring to God: Abraham (great Father), Eliab (my God is Father), Absalom (Father is security [peace]), Abijah (my Father is Yahweh), and many others. Moreover, (3) the idea of God as Father came to be used in interpreting the exodus from Egypt as the adoption of Israel as the son of God (Exodus 4:22–23; Hosea 11:1–4). The directness and intimacy of Jesus' consistent address of God as Father, however, seem to be distinctive. It is not by chance that his prayer begins, "Our Father in heaven. . ." (Matthew 6:9).

We cannot deny that the address of God as "Father" reflects the mores of patriarchal societies from which both Testaments come. Some therefore prefer to translate *pater* and *abba* with the gender-neutral term "Parent." Whether our churches will gradually move to gender-inclusive language in addressing God remains to be seen. In any case, the intimacy of familial language is a necessary balance to the austerity of references to the transcendent creator of all that is.

To speak of God as Parent or Father or Mother is to assume that God has personhood (not "is *a* person"). Is this pure metaphor? Does it describe reality? How can we grasp the idea that the ground of all being, the spiritual force behind all atoms and molecules of the universe, can be addressed as person? Let us leave room for mystery in our spirituality and give up trying to understand what is by definition beyond our reach. Let us be content with the ancient confession, "I believe in God the Father almighty, creator of heaven and earth."

God as Sustainer and Protector

The Apostles' Creed asserts that the almighty God is the creator of heaven and earth, but it says nothing explicit about God's continuing care for the creation—and for us humans. Are we to believe—as did the intellectuals called "Deists," among whom were many of the "founding fathers" of the United States—that God set the universe in motion and then sat back to see what would become of it? Does God intervene in the natural course of things? Does God care? These are difficult and perennial questions for persons of faith.

With the possible exception of the books of Ecclesiastes (which suggests that the ways of God are veiled from humans) and Esther (which completely avoids any mention of God), the Bible consistently affirms and presupposes that God cares for people. The essential character of God, according to numerous psalms (Psalm 146 is a good example) is "steadfast love," the translation of a Hebrew word (*hesed*) that can mean goodness, mercy, grace, fidelity, faithfulness, kindness, devotion, beauty, and compassionate love, among other things. Men and women of both Testaments offered up fervent prayers to the One they believed could defend them from foes and protect them from evil. Jesus also taught his disciples that God watches over not only human beings but even the birds of the air and the grass of the field (Matthew 6:25–30).

If God cares, and if God is almighty, why do suffering and grief come into our lives? This is one of the most difficult questions we humans can ask. Why do bad things happen, especially when they are apparently undeserved? A nonbeliever has little reason to think that things should balance out in this world, but the Christian person faces what seems to be an unsolvable dilemma. If God is good, just, and powerful, why has evil not been eliminated? In the final analysis, this question proves to be unanswerable. But there are some significant things that can be said about it from the biblical tradition.

"Evil" is a general term for all that is less than perfect in this world and in this life. It refers to everything that detracts from, distorts, or destroys the goodness that God wants for all people and for the whole creation. There are different kinds of evil. Natural disasters like tornadoes, tsunamis, earthquakes, and floods affect thousands of people each year. Evil can also come from society, such as war, discrimination, and poverty. And it can be personal, ranging from insults and theft to murder. We live in a fallen world; none of us is yet free from the experience of evil. We can scarcely believe that evil in any form comes from God, since what God creates is perfect. How, then, should we consider the question of evil in relation to the providence of God? Four things seem clear:

- Evil is a reality in our world and in our life. It cannot be ignored or wished away. If we are to have any peace in this world, we must face the fact that evil exists and learn how to deal with tragedy, sin, disappointment, and suffering. That most certainly is easier said than done.

- Not everything that happens on this earth is the will of God. Jesus taught us to pray, "Your will be done, on earth as it is in heaven" (Matthew 6:10). That reminds us that God's will is not now being done perfectly, and we pray for the time when it will be implemented on earth. Jesus taught that tragedies come upon people without regard to the degree of their sinfulness (Luke 13:1–5), and we therefore cannot rest with the idea that evil is punishment from God. Paul believed that God would ultimately destroy all evil powers (1 Corinthians 15:24–26).

- God struggles with us against evil. Jesus' ministry on earth was part of God's work against disease, sin, sickness, despair, and other evils. When we experience suffering, let us remember that God works on our side (Romans 8:28).

- In the end God will be victorious over evil, as Paul forcefully reminds us in 1 Corinthians 15:26–28. And Revelation, the last book of the Bible, ends with a glorious vision of God's final victory over evil:

See, the home of God is among mortals.
He will dwell with them;
they will be his peoples,
and God himself will be with them;
he will wipe every tear from their eyes.
Death will be no more;
mourning and crying and pain will be no more,
for the former things have passed away.
(Revelation 21:3–4)

Coins and currency of the United States proclaim, "In God we trust." Do we? Trust presupposes belief, and the object of our trust indicates where we place our confidence and our hope for the future. Can we say that most folks in Western society, including North America, look to the God of the Bible as the source of their personal or communal hope? There are many contenders for our attention and our ambitions, and the demands of contemporary life are heavy. To confess faith in God the Father almighty is to be able to pray with the psalmist:

> Whom have I in heaven but you?
> > And there is nothing on earth that I desire other than
> > you.
> My flesh and my heart may fail,
> > but God is the strength of my heart and my portion
> > forever.
> > > > > > (Psalm 73:25–26)

3

I Believe in Jesus Christ,
God's Only Son, Our Lord

MORE BOOKS HAVE BEEN WRITTEN about Jesus than about anyone else in history, and no one has been the focus of more debate, including in our mass media. Who is Jesus? Almost all possible answers have been given to this question. Over the centuries different persons have called him the Messiah, a martyr, a good human being, God-made-flesh, a miracle worker, a fraud, the suffering servant, a false teacher, redeemer of the world, a mystic, a philosopher, a magician, a prophet, a teacher of morality, a "new age" spiritualist, a reformer—and much more. Our creed, however, makes four affirmations about his identity: (1) his given name is Jesus; (2) he is the Christ; (3) he is the only Son of the Creator; and (4) for believers he is the Lord. Let us consider each of these in turn.

Jesus

The name *Jesus* in its English-language form comes from the Greek version of the Hebrew name *Joshua*, which means "Yahweh is salvation." The name Jesus was fairly commonly used in New Testament times. For example, the book of Sirach in the Apocrypha was written by "Jesus son of Sirach" (Jesus ben Sira).

Both Matthew and Luke assert that an angel commanded that Mary's son be given this name. According to Matthew 1:20–21, an anonymous angel appeared to Joseph and said, "Joseph, son of David, do not be afraid to take Mary as your wife, for the child conceived in her is from the Holy Spirit. She will bear a son, and you are to name him Jesus, for he will save his people from their sins." This writer is aware of the meaning of the Hebrew form of the name Jesus, and he links this meaning to the redemptive death of Jesus, which centers on his "blood . . . poured out for many for the forgiveness of sins" (Matthew 26:28).

In Luke 1:26–33 the angel is named Gabriel; he informs Mary (not Joseph) of her imminent pregnancy and of how the child is to be named: "You will conceive in your womb and bear a son, and you will name him Jesus" (verse 31). Joseph fulfills the command regarding naming in Matthew 1:25. Unlike Matthew, Luke reveals no awareness of the meaning of the name Jesus, but Luke also includes the fulfillment of the angel's words: Eight days after Jesus' birth, "it was time to circumcise the child; and he was called Jesus, the name given by the angel before he was conceived in the womb" (Luke 2:21).

Christ

"Christ" (Greek, *christos*) is a translation of the Hebrew Messiah (*mashiach*), "anointed." In the Old Testament, priests and kings were anointed with oil at the time they took office (for example, David's anointing is described in 1 Samuel 16:13). The Old Testament line of kings came to an end with the destruction of Judah by the Babylonians in 587 B.C. Many persons, however, hoped for the renewal of the monarchy and a new "anointed one"—a "Messiah." The hallmarks of the ideal Messiah are described in Isaiah 9:2–7 and 11:1–5. In these two poems, the Messiah would (1) be descended from David, the king par excellence; (2) conquer the enemies of Israel in a decisive battle; and (3) establish a universal kingdom of peace and justice for all. (Note that the enigmatic figure of the "Suffering Servant" of Isaiah 42:1–4; 49:1–6; 50:4–11; and 52:13—53:12 is not an anointed one and has a function completely different from that of the Davidic Messiah.)

Christians from the earliest times proclaimed Jesus to be "Messiah," or, from the Greek, "Christ." The word "Christ" even came to be used as Jesus' surname—already in Paul's letters (for example, Romans 1:1, 6, 7). Why and how the earliest Christians applied to Jesus a title that seemed to fit his activity so little is a difficult question. Several New Testament writers (for example, Matthew 1:1–17; Luke 3:31; and possibly Mark 10:47) claim that Jesus was descended from David. But Jesus never entertained a military role for himself, and he appears to have had little interest in what we call politics (with a few possible exceptions, like the statement about paying taxes to the emperor, Mark 12:13–17). Jesus was not a warrior, and he did not attempt to set up an earthly kingdom. Some early Christians applied to Jesus the idea of a "suffering Messiah," an idea that appears to have been entirely unknown to any group in Judaism at the time of the origin of Christianity and would be considered by Judaism a contradiction in terms. (The death of "my son the Messiah" in 2 Esdras [4 Ezra] 7:29, written at the end of the first century A.D., is no exception;

this refers to the natural death, not interpreted as redemptive, of a human being.)

The paradoxical aspect of giving Jesus the honorary title "Messiah" can be seen in a pivotal passage in the Gospel of Mark. Mark 8:27–38, known as "Peter's Confession," functions as a turning point in that Gospel. On the way to Caesarea Philippi, at the foot of Mount Hermon in the northeast corner of a Jewish settlement in Palestine, Mark reports that Jesus asked his disciples two questions. To the first, "Who do people say that I am?" the disciples respond with the same list Mark had given in 6:14–16 (John the Baptist, Elijah, one of the prophets). The second question is directed to the Twelve, "But who do you say that I am?" In Mark, Peter responds, "You are the Messiah" (Greek: *christos*). Up to this point in Mark, not one—not even the demons—had expressed such a thought. Nor did there appear to be a reason to think that Jesus of Nazareth was a messianic figure—one who would revive the Davidic kingdom by conducting military campaigns.

Mark's report of Jesus' response to Peter's confession is equally startling. First, Jesus "sternly ordered them not to tell anyone about him" (8:30). Then Jesus made an astounding announcement, his first "passion prediction": he "must undergo great suffering, and be rejected . . . and be killed" (8:31). Peter privately rebuked Jesus for these thoughts, but Jesus turned to the other disciples and rebuked Peter in the harshest language: "Get behind me, Satan! For you are setting your mind not on divine things but on human things" (8:33). He then told his disciples to be prepared to take up their cross (8:34).

Whatever Mark thought that Peter had in mind when he confessed Jesus to be the Messiah, it did not involve the idea of Jesus' imminent suffering and death. Did Mark attribute to Peter the traditional concept of messiahship in Jewish sources—a Davidic warrior—which Jesus rejected for himself? Did Jesus repudiate Peter's understanding of Jesus?

The conclusion must remain unsatisfactory. We cannot know precisely why the early Christians called Jesus the Messiah (Christ), but it is clear that they found his kingship to be other than a geographical realm on earth: "My kingdom is not from this world" (John 18:36).

Son of God

The idea of sonship with God is found in three contexts in the Old Testament.

- Israel as a people becomes God's "firstborn son" at the exodus from Egypt (Exodus 4:22), a thought taken up by later prophets: "Out of Egypt I called my son" (Hosea 11:1; see also Jeremiah 31:20).

- The Israelite king was honored as a son of God, a conception that goes back to the prophet Nathan's oracle given to David in 2 Samuel 7:14, according to which God "will be a father to him, and he shall be a son to me." Psalm 2 was chanted by the temple singers at the enthronement of a king, who says, "I will tell of the decree of the LORD: He said to me, 'You are my son; today I have begotten you'" (verse 7). This seems to be the Israelite version of the widespread ancient conception of divine kingship.

- Angelic or heavenly beings, members of God's court, are "sons of God" (Genesis 6:2; Job 1:6; 2:1; 38:7; Psalm 29:1; 89:6; in the NRSV many of these passages are translated as "heavenly beings"). The "children of the

Most High" in Psalm 82:6 are the gods of the nations surrounding Israel, and they all "shall die like mortals" (verse 7).

The Old Testament concept of divine sonship is one of honor and dignity. It carries with it the ideas of election by God and the resulting responsibility for implementing God's will in the life of the people. But did the New Testament writers draw on the Old Testament usage of the phrase "son of God"?

Christians applied the complementary titles Messiah and Son of God to Jesus from the earliest years. Mark gives his Gospel the title, "The beginning of the good news of Jesus *Christ*, the *Son of God*" (Mark 1:1, italics mine). Matthew begins his Gospel by reflecting on *how* Jesus is Messiah (through his ancestry, Matthew 1:1–17) and Son of God (through his birth from a virgin, Matthew 1:18–25). The Gospel of John culminates with the combination of these two titles: "These are written so that you may come to believe that Jesus is the Messiah, the Son of God, and that through believing you may have life in his name" (20:31). According to Mark, which is the earliest written Gospel, Jesus becomes aware of his sonship with God at his baptism by John ("You [singular pronoun] are my Son, the Beloved," Mark 1:11). But, although the demons recognize Jesus' sonship (Mark 3:11; 5:7), the disciples first learn of this at the Transfiguration ("This is my Son, the Beloved," Mark 9:7). Later Gospels, especially John, describe Jesus as making explicit claims to unique sonship with God. (On Jesus' address of God as "Father," see chapter 2, above.)

When we consider the New Testament writings in their probable chronological order, we can see a reverse progression with respect to the confession of Jesus as the Son of God. Paul, writing in about 56 A.D., but seemingly quoting an earlier passage, says that Jesus was "declared to be Son of God . . . by resurrection from the dead" (Romans 1:4). Mark, the earliest Gospel, written around 70 A.D., traces this designation back to Jesus' baptism (Mark 1:11; see above). Matthew and Luke, writing a little later than Mark, antedate this further, calling Jesus Son of God from the time of his birth (Matthew 1:20; Luke 1:32, 35), while John traces Jesus' divine glory to the "beginning" (before creation; John 1:1).

The creed adds a significant word to our confession of Jesus' divine sonship: he is God's "only" Son. In some sense, all believers are children of God, and Jesus asked his disciples to call God "Our Father," just as he did. Moreover, Paul emphasizes that baptism unites us with the death and resurrection of Jesus, making us his brothers and sisters—and thereby children of God (Galatians 4:4–7; Romans 8:14–18). In our creed, however, we acknowledge Jesus as the unique, the *only* Son of God. Once again it is clear that ancient beliefs necessitated this emphasis. (1) The Greeks were familiar with miracle workers known as "divine men," persons who possessed special powers. Moreover, in the Roman world, emperors were typically called "sons of God" (*divi filius*). Neither Greeks nor Romans drew a sharp distinction between human and divine. (2) The Gnostics of the second century presupposed a great chasm between the transcendent, supreme God and the material world in which we live. Bridging this gap, they speculated, were "emanations," "aeons," or "archons" that issued forth from the spiritual realm; some Gnostic cults imagined that there were as many as 365 such beings. Among these, the Gnostics thought, might be the "Logos," which came to be the term for the divine aspect of Jesus as the Christ. Therefore, when the Christians confessed Jesus to be the "only Son" of "God the Father almighty, creator of heaven and earth," they emphatically and categorically denied that there were any other mediators between

God and humankind. In distinction from all divine miracle workers, divine emperors, and semidivine new-age emanations, Jesus,
they confessed, is the unique revealer of the one God.

Lord

Jesus, the creed insists, is "our Lord." There is now a connection between the Christ, the unique Son, and us. I mentioned in
chapter 1 above that the very oldest Christian creed is probably
the simple confession, "Jesus is Lord" (in Greek: *kyrios 'Iesous*; 1
Corinthians 12:3). This goes back to the earliest believers, who
applied the Aramaic word *Mar*, "Lord," to Jesus, including in the
prayer "Maranatha," which means "Our Lord, come!" (1 Corinthians 16:22; see also Revelation 22:20).

The Greek term for "Lord" is *kyrios*. In Greek culture, it could
be a simple term of address, comparable to "Sir," as when the Syro-
phoenician woman calls Jesus "*kyrios*" in Mark 7:28 (this meaning is found also in Matthew 13:27; 21:30; Luke 13:8; 14:22; John
4:11; 9:36; 12:21; and elsewhere). Quite differently, *kyrios* in the
Greek Old Testament translates the Hebrew name for God, "Yahweh." The term was common also in the Graeco-Roman world as
a designation of pagan gods, as Paul indicates in 1 Corinthians
8:5–6: "Even though there may be so-called gods in heaven or on
earth—as in fact there are many gods and many lords—yet for
us there is one God, the Father . . . and one Lord, Jesus Christ."
When early Christians confessed that Jesus was their Lord, they
deliberately rejected the many lords in their milieu and, at some
personal risk, challenged also the claims to dominion on the part
of the secular rulers.

Paul, in Philippians 2:9–11, calls *kyrios* "the name that is
above every name," which God gave to Jesus in his resurrection-

exaltation. Every creature, whether in heaven or on earth, should ultimately "confess that Jesus Christ is Lord [*kyrios*], to the glory of God the Father" (verse 11). (The outrageous idea, which continues to be set forth by some interpreters, that Paul here applies the name *Yahweh* to the risen Jesus is categorically excluded by the explicit statement that, by confessing Jesus as *kyrios*, we give glory to "God the Father." Paul deliberately distinguished between Jesus and God the Father, even stating in 1 Corinthians 15:28 that ultimately "the Son himself will also be subjected to the one who put all things in subjection under him, so that God may be all in all." Paul often used trinitarian language, but he seems to have envisioned the ultimate absorption of even those distinctions into the oneness and fullness of God.)

To call Jesus "Lord" is to testify that our lives are oriented around Jesus and his teaching about the will of God for our lives. We announce that we take his suffering, death, and resurrection as the model for life in this world and the basis of our hope for the next. To confess Jesus as "our Lord" is to put our priorities in proper order.

With our confession that Jesus Christ, our Lord, is the *only* Son of the Father, we touch on the exclusivist aspect of our faith, the claim that one individual man who lived in an identifiable place at a specific time is uniquely related to God and is our Lord. We approach God through his only Son. When we speak these words, however, we are not saying anything about someone else's beliefs or the lack thereof; we are giving witness to what *we* believe and to the nature of our approach to God.

4

He Was Conceived
by the Holy Spirit
and Born of the Virgin Mary

THE SECOND ARTICLE of the Apostles' Creed affirms what we are to believe about the birth of Jesus, how he came to die, and what happened to him after his death. In this chapter I consider what we can know about Jesus' birth and death, and how this relates to our lives as believers.

The Birth Narratives

The conception and birth of Jesus are narrated in the New Testament in only two places, the first two chapters of Matthew and the first two chapters of Luke. Notice first the general outline of each:

Matthew	*Luke*
The ancestry of Jesus through Joseph back to Abraham and David (1:1–17).	The conception of John the Baptist by Elizabeth (1:5–25).
An anonymous angel informs Joseph of Mary's pregnancy; the child is born; Joseph names him "Jesus" (1:18–25).	The angel Gabriel informs Mary that she will become pregnant; she is to name the child "Jesus" (1:26–38).
Wise men from the east pay homage to the child in the "house" (presumably Joseph's) in Bethlehem (2:1–12).	Mary visits Elizabeth and sings the *Magnificat* (1:39–56).
Warned by an angel, Joseph takes the child and his mother to Egypt (2:13–15).	Birth of John the Baptist; his father, Zechariah, sings the *Benedictus* (1:57–80).
In a furious rage, King Herod kills all boys up to two years of age in the area of Bethlehem (2:16–18).	Joseph and Mary travel from Nazareth to Bethlehem, where Jesus is born; shepherds in the area rejoice and praise God (2:1–20).
After Herod's death, Joseph leaves Egypt with his family and settles in Nazareth in Galilee, not back to his home in Bethlehem (2:19–23).	Jesus is named, circumcised, and presented at the Temple; Simeon and Anna praise God (2:21–38).

In Matthew, Joseph is prominent. He deliberates on how to respond to Mary's pregnancy, and the angel encourages him to take Mary as his wife and to name the child. Jesus is born in Joseph's "house" in Bethlehem (2:11). An astrological phenomenon leads wise men (magi) from Persia (Iran) to seek the newborn "King of the Jews" at Herod's court in Jerusalem. They find the child in the house in Bethlehem. An angel again appears to Joseph, warning him to flee from Herod's jealous rage. The holy family moves to Egypt. Herod murders the male children of Bethlehem. When Herod dies, Joseph returns to Israel but, because Herod's son Archelaus ruled Judea, they went to live in Nazareth in Galilee, instead of Bethlehem.

In Luke, Mary is prominent and Joseph remains in the background. The angel—here named Gabriel—appears to Mary. Joseph and Mary live in Nazareth, and Jesus happens to be born in Bethlehem only because the Roman emperor decreed that everyone had to be registered in "their own towns" (2:3). Shepherds from the fields rejoice over the newborn son, but no wise men come to pay homage. And Luke is careful to assure the reader that Jesus' parents performed all the duties and ceremonies prescribed by Jewish law and tradition.

More striking than all these differences of detail, however, is the contrast in literary style. Matthew writes chapters 1–2 brusquely, always with an eye on passages from the Old Testament that relate to the sequence of his narrative:

- The genealogy in 1:1–17 draws on statements in Genesis and 1 Chronicles 1–9.
- Matthew 1:23, "the virgin shall conceive," cites the Greek translation of Isaiah 7:14.
- Matthew 2:6, "You, O Bethlehem . . . from you shall come a ruler," cites Micah 5:2.
- Matthew 2:15, "Out of Egypt I have called my son," cites Hosea 11:1.

- Matthew 2:18, "Rachel weeping for her children," reflects Jeremiah 31:15.
- Matthew 2:23, "He will be called a Nazorean," is not an exact quotation of any Old Testament passage, although "Nazorean" is close to the Hebrew word translated "branch" in Isaiah 11:1.

In addition, Matthew 2 makes several allusions to the story of Moses' birth in Exodus 2. Luke also is heavily imbued with Old Testament piety. In contrast to Matthew, however, Luke draws on its classic poetry to create four striking and memorable pieces of Christian poetry:

- Mary's *Magnificat* (1:46–55) has several allusions to the Song of Hannah in 1 Samuel 2:1–10.
- Zechariah's *Benedictus* (1:68–79) draws on phrases from Psalms 18:1–3; 92:10–11; 132:17–18; Malachi 4:2, 5; and elsewhere.
- The shepherds' *Gloria* (2:14).
- Simeon's *Nunc Dimittis* (2:29–32) alludes to Isaiah 42:6; 49:6; 52:10.

Each of these Lukan poems has gained a worthy place in Christian liturgy.

What, then, do the birth stories in Matthew and Luke have in common? They agree on the names of Jesus, Joseph, and Mary; that he was born in Bethlehem of Judea; that he grew up in Nazareth of Galilee; and—significantly, because it is presupposed—that he was born before Herod the Great died early in 4 B.C. We have scarcely any other information about the date of Jesus' birth, but the years 6–4 B.C. generally agree with what Luke tells us about the year Jesus began his ministry and about his age at that time. Luke 3:23 asserts that "Jesus was about thirty years old when he began his work," and Luke dates the ministry of John the Baptist to the "fifteenth year of the reign of Emperor Tiberius, when Pontius Pilate was governor of Judea" (3:1). Tiberius was emperor from 14–37 A.D.; the fifteenth year would be approximately 28 A.D., depending on how you count partial years. Pontius Pilate was governor of Judea from 26–36 A.D. Jesus' ministry presumably began shortly after John's, probably in 29 or 30 A.D. (See also below on the date of Jesus' death.)

Conceived by the Holy Spirit

All of our New Testament Gospels assert that God's Spirit directed Jesus' ministry of preaching, teaching, and healing. Mark reports that, at his baptism, Jesus "saw the heavens torn apart and the Spirit descending like a dove on him" (1:10). The author of the Gospel of John seems to be aware of this tradition when he reports that the baptizer testified, "I saw the Spirit descending from heaven like a dove, and it remained on him" (1:32). Matthew and Luke, however, trace Jesus' Spirit-filled life back to the moment of his conception. According to Matthew 1:20, an angel assuages Joseph's anxiety about Mary's pregnancy: "Joseph, son of David, do not be afraid to take Mary as your wife, for the child conceived in her is from the Holy Spirit" (see also verse 18). In Luke, when Mary wonders how she could conceive as a virgin, the angel Gabriel assures her, "The Holy Spirit will come upon you, and the power of the Most High will overshadow you; therefore the child to be born will be holy; he will be called Son of God" (1:35). Jesus, as our creed has it, was "conceived by the Holy Spirit."

Matthew and Luke do not explain how we are to understand that Mary conceived by the Holy Spirit. Both Gospel writers, however, link this idea to the Christian confession of Jesus as God's Son: they answer the question of *how* Jesus could be God's unique Son by referring to his unique conception by the power of the Spirit of God. Luke expressly states this in 1:35, and Matthew asserts that the Spirit-conception of Jesus means that Jesus will be called Emmanuel, "God is with us" (1:23). This means that the essential idea of the doctrine of the virginal conception of Jesus is that Jesus' birth resulted from the express will of God for the "salvation . . . prepared in the presence of all peoples, a light for revelation to the Gentiles and for glory to your people Israel" (Luke 2:30–32).

Born of the Virgin Mary

Although Jesus' birth is narrated in the New Testament only in the first two chapters of Matthew and Luke, Paul makes a passing reference to it in Galatians 4:4–5: "God sent his Son, born of a woman, born under the law, in order to redeem those who were under the law." Paul, however, nowhere mentions the name of Jesus' mother, but his contacts with Jesus' brother James (Acts 15:2, 13; 21:18; 1 Corinthians 15:7; Galatians 1:19) leave open the possibility that he had some knowledge of Jesus' early life. In Romans 1:3 Paul mentions Jesus' descent "from David according to the flesh," although we cannot tell from this whether he had Joseph or Mary in mind (both of the genealogies of Jesus, Matthew 1:1–17 and Luke 3:23–38, trace his Davidic ancestry back through Joseph.)

Most Christians today commemorate the conception of Jesus nine months before Christmas, that is, on March 25, the "annunciation of our Lord," so called because of Luke's story of the angel Gabriel's announcement to Mary of her pregnancy

(Luke 1:26–38). Matthew and Luke, as noted above, assert that Mary conceived while still a virgin. Matthew 1:22–23 takes this to "fulfill" the Greek text of Isaiah 7:14, "The virgin shall conceive and bear a son," even though the original Hebrew of Isaiah uses the word for "young woman" rather than "virgin." The same thought is expressed in more poetic language in Luke 1:34–35 (see above).

Early Christians had great respect for Mary, and this veneration increased as the decades and centuries passed. In the second century the church fathers Justin Martyr and Irenaeus of Lyons called her the "New Eve," corresponding to Jesus as the "last Adam" (see 1 Corinthians 15:45). Then, from the early third century, beginning with the church father Origen (approximately 185–254 A.D.), Mary was often given the Greek title *theotokos*, "bearer of God," commonly rendered in English as "Mother of God." The Council of Chalcedon in 451 A.D. condemned anyone who would refuse this title to Mary. Among the Protestant reformers of the sixteenth century, Martin Luther was perhaps the most devoted to Mary, and he enthusiastically applied the title *theotokos* to her.

"Conceived by the Spirit" and "of the virgin" point to the two aspects of Jesus as the Christ that came to be more clearly elaborated and codified in later creeds. Jesus, "born of a woman," is fully human and, as "conceived by the Spirit," is uniquely related to God. Thus Martin Luther in his Small Catechism began the explanation of the second article of the creed with the words, "I believe that Jesus Christ, true God, begotten of the Father in eternity, and also a true human being, born of the virgin Mary, is my

Lord." As we speak the words of the creed, we confess that Jesus, being conceived by God's Spirit, is uniquely related to God and, as the human son of Mary, is able to bring us unique salvation.

5

He Suffered . . . Was Crucified, Died, and Was Buried

ALTHOUGH ALL FOUR GOSPELS place the crucifixion on a Friday at Passover time, the Gospel of John additionally asserts that, in the year of Jesus' crucifixion, the Passover began on Friday evening, after Jesus' death, thus coinciding with the Sabbath. This is clearly stated in John 18:28 (and also in John 19:42): the disciples did not enter Pilate's headquarters "so as to avoid ritual defilement and to be able to eat the Passover." Presumably, the thought is that Jews who entered a Gentile area before the Passover meal would be ritually polluted. (In John 13 the last supper of Jesus with his disciples is not a Passover meal. There is no mention of bread and wine there; instead, John brings in the story of Jesus washing his disciples' feet.)

Passover was calculated as falling soon after the first full moon after the spring equinox (which most often occurs in our calendar on March 21). Projecting backward from our calendar, it is highly probable that Passover coincided with the Sabbath in 30 A.D. This date for Jesus' crucifixion fits with the chronological statements in Luke 3:1 (especially that the work of John the Baptist began "in the fifteenth year of the reign of Emperor Tiberius," that is, about 28 A.D.). It is consistent also with the early date at which Paul joined the Jesus movement (about 32 A.D.) and with the years of the term of Pontius Pilate as governor or prefect of Judea (26–36 A.D.). That Jesus died at 3:00 P.M. is confirmed by Mark 15:34 and the parallels in Matthew 27:46 and Luke 23:44. Therefore, if we accept John's statement that the Passover in the year of the crucifixion began on Friday evening, we might conclude that Jesus died at 3:00 P.M. on Friday, April 7, in 30 A.D. (reading from our calendar back into antiquity).* Because of the confusing array of calendars in use in antiquity, however, and the discrepancies between John and the other Gospels, we cannot be dogmatic about this date.

The Path to Golgotha

The story of Jesus' death, the "passion narrative," occupies a significant part of each of the four Gospels (Matthew 26–27; Mark 14–15; Luke 22–23; John 18–19). But *why* was Jesus executed? To

---

*Disagreement among scholars can be seen in two classic works: (1) Charles Guignebert, *Jesus* (translated by S. H. Hooke; New York: Knopf, 1935), pages 421–427. In note 3 on page 426 Guignebert points out that Nisan 14 (the day in the Jewish calendar on which Passover begins in the evening) fell on Friday, April 7, in the year 30 and on Friday, April 3, in the year 33. He notes also, however, that there is much about which we are uncertain with respect to ancient Jewish calendars. (2) Maurice Goguel, in *The Life of Jesus* (translated by Olive

say that it was the will of God is a theological statement and does not explain why the Jewish authorities in Jerusalem turned him over to Pilate for judgment. On this historical question it is crucial to distinguish the motivations of the Jewish authorities from the thinking of Pontius Pilate, the Roman prefect—a Gentile. Each Gospel depicts ways in which Jesus' ministry evoked opposition from various groups. There are examples of rising hostility in Mark, the earliest written Gospel that we have. In Mark, scribes accuse Jesus of committing blasphemy by arrogating to himself the divine privilege of forgiving sins (Mark 2:7). Some Pharisees accuse him of having table fellowship with sinners (Mark 2:16) and of breaking the Sabbath laws (Mark 2:24; 3:2). Scribes from Jerusalem accuse him of working with Beelzebul (Mark 3:22). Pharisees accuse him of not following the food laws (Mark 7:1–2 and especially verses 18–19). At the council of "the high priest, all the chief priests, the elders, and the scribes" (Mark 14:53, 55) that passed judgment on Jesus before his death, however, only two charges are made. First, certain "false" witnesses testified, "We heard him say, 'I will destroy this temple that is made with hands, and in three days I will build another, not made with hands'" (Mark 14:58). This same Gospel writer had reported in 13:1–2 that Jesus had, in fact, predicted the destruction of the temple (which actually occurred at the hands of the Roman army in the summer of 70 A.D.). But according to Mark, Jesus had not said that *he* would destroy the temple. The other charge at the council of Jewish authorities was blasphemy, which, in Mark 14:61–64, resulted from Jesus' response to the high priest, an affirmation

Wyon; New York: Macmillan, 1944), pages 223–232, arrives at a different conclusion, asserting that we can "consider it as an established fact that Jesus died during the Passover of the year 28" (page 228). Goguel's early dating, however, is far from certain.

that he was "the Messiah, the Son of the Blessed One," and that the high priest would "see the Son of Man . . . 'coming with the clouds of heaven.'" Although it is impossible to reconstruct the course of this conflict in detail, it is clear that—to speak in general terms—the Jewish authorities in Jerusalem viewed Jesus as a false teacher.

But what interest would Pilate have in a Jewish false teacher? None whatsoever. Mark's account makes abundantly clear that the Jewish authorities handed Jesus to Pilate as a messianic pretender, a political threat. Pilate wants to know whether Jesus thinks he is "King of the Jews." Pilate offers the crowd the release of Jesus or Barabbas, a political insurrectionist (Mark 15:7). Jesus is mocked by the Roman soldiers—"Hail, King of the Jews!"— clothed in purple, and crowned with thorns (Mark 15:17–20). And on his cross is written the reason the Romans crucified him; it read simply, "The King of the Jews" (Mark 15:26). To use modern terms, the religious charges at the Jewish council became political charges when Jesus appeared before the Romans. All accounts, however, agree that Pilate issued the death sentence, and Jesus suffered a Roman form of execution, crucifixion. This death was typically the sentence passed on criminals, rebels, and fugitive slaves. It was intended to be slow and painful, and the victims were lifted up in public places, like crossroads or busy thoroughfares. It was death of utter ignominy.

The Four Verbs

Many persons have wondered why the creed emphasizes the passion and death of Jesus in a seemingly redundant way by the use of four verbs: "suffered . . . crucified . . . died . . . buried." Who would deny the sufferings and death of Jesus? The answer at first glance is surprising: a number of Gnostic cults in the second and third centuries did precisely that. Presupposing that the Supreme God was revealed in Jesus, and presupposing also that the Supreme God had nothing to do with the creation or preservation of this material world, to the Gnostics it seemed blasphemous to believe in the historical reality of the death of the Redeemer. Thus a certain Cerinthus, who lived in Ephesus toward the end of the first century, distinguished between the man Jesus, the human son of Joseph and Mary, and the divine Christ, who descended on Jesus at the time of his baptism. Before Jesus' death, the divine Christ abandoned Jesus to his fate. Similarly, the Gospel of Peter has Jesus cry on the cross, "My power, my power, why have you forsaken me?"—the cry of the man Jesus forsaken by the divine Christ. Another Gnostic, Basilides, who flourished at Alexandria, Egypt, between 120 and 140 A.D., taught that the Father had sent his only Son to rouse the divine spark that was latent within some human beings. But the Son's task did not involve suffering; according to Basilides, Simon of Cyrene and not Jesus was crucified. Several other Gnostic leaders taught that Jesus had no material body; he only seemed to have one. His supposed crucifixion, therefore, was no more than an illusion. No Gnostic would confess that Jesus "suffered under Pontius Pilate, was crucified, died, and was buried." The formulation of the creed was designed to draw a line between Gnostics and other believers, and it did so effectively.

The creed asserts what we all now take as established fact: Jesus' death was an actual historical event. This death, moreover, was a great trauma for the earliest Christians: the revered teacher had been executed as a criminal by orders of the Roman governor. How could this have happened? Had God abandoned Jesus, the faithful servant? Could there be such a thing as a crucified Messiah? The crucifixion had to be interpreted, and the earliest disciples combed through the Scriptures, the Old Testament, to find answers. No wonder that the death of Jesus occupied a central place in Christian preaching from the beginning. (On the death of Jesus as redemptive, see chapter 10, "The Forgiveness of Sins," below.)

Buried

The first Christian writer whose works have survived—Paul—explicitly mentions that Jesus was buried. In a creed-like passage, Paul indicates that his information about the death and resurrection of Jesus antedates his writing. It was given to him:

> I handed on to you as of first importance what I in turn had received: that Christ died for our sins in accordance with the scriptures, and that he was buried, and that he was raised on the third day in accordance with the scriptures. (1 Corinthians 15:3–4)

In a graphic passage, Paul asserts that

> all of us who have been baptized into Christ Jesus were baptized into his death. Therefore we have been buried with him by baptism into death, so that as Christ was raised from the dead by the glory of the Father, so we too might walk in newness of life. (Romans 6:3–4; the same thought occurs in Colossians 2:12).

For Paul, the image of the baptized person descending into the water was a reenactment of the burial of Jesus; it accomplished—perhaps in a quasi-mystical sense—the union of the believer with Jesus.

All four New Testament Gospels offer a narrative of Jesus' burial (Mark 15:42–47; Matthew 27:57–61; Luke 23:50–56; John

19:38–42). In all accounts, the man who buried Jesus was Joseph of Arimathea, described by Mark as "a respected member of the council, who was also himself waiting expectantly for the kingdom of God" (15:43; Luke is similar). Matthew (27:57) and John (19:38) add that this Joseph was a disciple of Jesus (John adds, "though a secret one because of his fear of the Jews"). John is the only writer who brings Nicodemus into the scene. All agree that Joseph laid the body of Jesus in a rock-hewn tomb, and Matthew adds that it was "his own new tomb" (27:60). Christians at Jerusalem had strong traditions about the location of this tomb and, when Emperor Constantine's mother, Helena, visited Palestine in 326 A.D., she identified the place of Jesus' burial and resurrection at what is now the Church of the Holy Sepulchre in Jerusalem. This tradition has strong claims of historical authenticity.

Jesus' death is a real event, and it is at the same time a graphic symbol of all human suffering. According to Mark 15:34 and Matthew 27:46, Jesus' last words before his death were the "cry of dereliction," "My God, my God, why have you forsaken me?" (a quotation of Psalm 22:1). Some scholars have pointed out the striking contrast between the death of Socrates in Athens in the fifth century B.C. and the death of Jesus in first-century Palestine. Socrates died heroically and calmly, comforting his grieving friends and disciples with thoughts of the survival of the "soul" before drinking the hemlock. Jesus died with the terror of death. He endured his sufferings and his awful death, however, so that he, according to one anonymous early believer, might "free those who all their lives were held in slavery by the fear of death" (Hebrews 2:15).

6

The Great Omission:
Between Birth and Death

HAVE YOU EVER NOTICED the great omission in the Apostles' Creed? It says nothing whatever about the time between Jesus' birth and the day of his death. Why is this? Did the Christians who formulated this ancient creed find nothing in the ministry of Jesus that was worthy of mention? Were they uninterested in his teachings and his works of mercy? Did they restrict Christian faith to his miraculous birth, his innocent sufferings and death, and his exaltation to the presence of God? The answer is: quite certainly not! The explanation is more simple than that.

The great omission must be understood by recalling the anti-Gnostic origin of the Apostles' Creed. When the creed identifies the creator God as the Father of Jesus and insists on the reality of Jesus' physical sufferings and death, it draws a line between

Gnostics and other Christian believers. The Christians of the Apostles' Creed treasured the Gospels' reports of Jesus' ministry, and they found little in it to be controversial. Most Gnostics also valued the tradition of Jesus' teachings, even though they compiled distinctive—and often bizarre—collections of such. What Jesus taught was not a basic issue between the Gnostics and the other Christians.

To be sure, we find also in our New Testament Gospels a great omission. Only Luke includes anything about Jesus between his birth and his baptism by John—the story of the twelve-year-old Jesus in Jerusalem with his parents for the feast of Passover (Luke 2:41–52). This gap in the story led to the writing of several apocryphal Gospels in the second and third centuries that recount various miracles attributed to the boy Jesus, for example, the "Protevangelium of James." In addition we know the text of several dozen other Gospels that purport to contain the teachings of Jesus, including those attributed to Peter, Thomas, Philip, and several others. Apart from the birth stories in Matthew and Luke, however, all four Gospels of the New Testament begin their narratives with the account of Jesus' baptism by John. What, then, can we know or believe about the ministry of Jesus?

Some aspects of the outward events of Jesus' life are firmly grounded. As noted above, he was born a year or two before 4 B.C. He was a Galilean from Nazareth. On a trip south to Judea he was influenced by John the Baptist and was baptized. After John's arrest, Jesus began to preach in Galilee and gathered about himself a small group of loyal disciples, both men and women. He performed acts of healing and exorcism and preached good news to the downtrodden and oppressed. As Passover in 30 A.D. approached, he entered the temple in Jerusalem, protesting the arrangements for sacrifice and antagonizing many persons who were in authority. He was executed in Jerusalem by order of the Roman prefect Pontius Pilate. Within weeks of his death, his earliest followers proclaimed that God had raised him from the dead, taking him into the divine presence.

There is also clarity about the essential themes of Jesus' teaching. The starting point of Jesus' teaching was his certainty about the imminence of "the kingdom of God," that is, God's effective rule in this world. Thus the summary in Mark 1:14–15:

> Now after John was arrested, Jesus came into Galilee, proclaiming the good news of God, and saying, "The time is fulfilled, and the kingdom of God has come near; repent, and believe in the good news."

The fact that Jesus waited to begin his ministry until John's had come to an end suggests that Jesus viewed his own work as a continuation of John's, at least in some respects. The first statement, "the time is fulfilled," points to the eschatological component of Jesus' teaching. He assumed that history was about to enter a turning point. Jesus referred to the imminent implementation of God's struggle against evil as the nearness of God's kingdom. And the people were to prepare for this historical turn by repenting.

Jesus often introduced his parables with the words, "The kingdom of God is like. . . ." At his last meal with his disciples, he promised that he would "never again drink of the fruit of the vine until that day when I drink it new in the kingdom of God" (Mark 14:25; see also Matthew 8:11 and Luke 13:29). And he taught his disciples to pray, "Your kingdom come," which is tantamount to praying, "Your will be done, on earth as it is in heaven" (Matthew 6:10). Jesus, according to the New Testament Gospels, saw his healings as signs of God's rapidly increasing overcoming of the multifaceted forms of evil. He healed the blind, the deaf, the paralyzed, persons afflicted with fever, persons with a speech impediment, and others. Other "mighty works" attributed to Jesus are exorcisms and nature miracles, including the feeding of a multitude of persons with meager supplies.

If a historical turning point—the effective rule of God—is at hand, one that involves God's judgment on evil, how should one prepare for it? Here we find the function of Jesus' ethical teachings. They showed his hearers how to "repent" in view of the impending crisis. The in-breaking of God's kingdom, Jesus taught, would involve a great reversal. In a discussion with his disciples about the trauma of this turn in history, Jesus said, "Many who are first will be last, and the last will be first" (Mark 10:31; there are parallels in Matthew 19:30; 20:16; and Luke 13:30). The proud, those who rule over others, and the self-satisfied will find their fortunes reversed in the new age, while the humble poor, those who suffer illness, the oppressed, and those who cry out for justice will experience the fullness of God's blessings. Nowhere is this more compellingly expressed than in Jesus' Beatitudes. Compare the two versions of them, in Matthew and in Luke:

Matthew 5:3–12	*Luke 6:20–23*
Blessed are the poor in spirit, for theirs is the kingdom of heaven.	Blessed are you who are poor, for yours is the kingdom of God.
Blessed are those who mourn, for they will be comforted.	
Blessed are the meek, for they will inherit the earth.	

Blessed are those who hunger and thirst for righteousness, for they will be filled.	Blessed are you who are hungry now, for you will be filled.
	Blessed are you who weep now, for you will laugh.
Blessed are the merciful, for they will receive mercy.	
Blessed are the pure in heart, for they will see God.	
Blessed are the peacemakers, for they will be called children of God.	
Blessed are those who are persecuted for righteousness' sake, for theirs is the kingdom of heaven. Blessed are you when people revile you and persecute you . . . for your reward is great in heaven.	Blessed are you when people hate you, and when they exclude you, revile you, and defame you . . . for surely your reward is great in heaven.

Luke's form, in the second-person pronoun "you," is directed to the hearers, while Matthew puts the blessings in a more universal form, using the third-person pronoun, "theirs," "those who. . ." (except for the final sentence, "Blessed are you. . ."). In any case, these blessings are a terse summary of the virtues Jesus taught his followers. True repentance—preparation for the implementation of God's will on earth—involves practicing mercy, righteousness, and peace in our daily lives.

Jesus' moral teachings are encapsulated also in two classic statements (both of which have precedents in the words of other Jewish teachers). The first, about the greatest commandment, is transmitted in Matthew 22:34–40; Mark 12:28–34; and Luke 10:25–28. I cite the Markan passage:

> One of the scribes . . . asked him, "Which commandment is the first of all?" Jesus answered, "The first is, 'Hear, O Israel: the Lord our God, the Lord is one; you shall love the Lord your God with all your heart, and with all your soul, and with all your mind, and with all your strength.' The second is this, 'You shall love your neighbor as yourself.' There is no other commandment greater than these." Then the scribe said to him, "You are right, Teacher . . . this is much more important than all whole burnt offerings and sacrifices." When Jesus saw that he answered wisely, he said to him, "You are not far from the kingdom of God."

Jesus cites the "first commandment" from Deuteronomy 6:4–5, the foundational affirmation of Judaism to this day, and the second from Leviticus 19:18. Matthew 22:40 adds, "On these two commandments hang all the law and the prophets" (the Law and the Prophets are the first two major sections of the Hebrew Bible). If love of God and love of neighbor become the lodestar of our lives, all the rest is commentary. It is significant also that Mark links striving after these two commandments to nearness to the kingdom of God. To follow the two great commandments is to begin to implement God's will in our lives.

The second classic ethical statement in the teachings of Jesus is the "Golden Rule." It is found in its "negative" form, "Do not do to others what you do not want them to do to you," in several pre-Christian sources, including Confucius, *Analects* 12:2; 15:23 (approximately 500 B.C.), and Rabbi Hillel (late first century B.C. to early first century A.D.), Babylonian Talmud, *Shabbat* 31a. It is formulated in positive form in both Matthew and Luke:

Matthew 7:12	*Luke 6:31*
In everything do to others as you would have them do to you; for this is the law and the prophets.	Do to others as you would have them do to you.

Some persons have argued that the Golden Rule is not in itself sufficient as an ethical guide. For example, if you like rap music, are you obliged to play it in the presence of someone who prefers Bach? You would be hard pressed, however, to find a more noble or workable guiding principle for making moral decisions. It expresses in different words the command to love your neighbor as yourself.

Many persons speak disparagingly of those who consider Jesus to have been "only a teacher." Although it is clearly not the whole truth, Jesus was indeed a teacher and a prophet, and we neglect his moral advice at our peril. Even Paul, who "decided to know nothing among you [the Corinthians] except Jesus Christ, and him crucified" (1 Corinthians 2:2), was well aware of the importance for the believers of what Jesus preached during his brief ministry. He wrote to the Romans:

> Let love be genuine; hate what is evil, hold fast to what is good; love one another with mutual affection; outdo one another in showing honor. Do not lag in zeal, be ardent in spirit, serve the Lord. Rejoice in hope, be patient in

suffering, persevere in prayer. Contribute to the needs of the saints; extend hospitality to strangers.

Bless those who persecute you; bless and do not curse them. Rejoice with those who rejoice, weep with those who weep. Live in harmony with one another; do not be haughty, but associate with the lowly; do not claim to be wiser than you are. Do not repay anyone evil for evil, but take thought for what is noble in the sight of all. If it is possible, so far as it depends on you, live peaceably with all. Beloved, never avenge yourselves, but leave room for the wrath of God; for it is written, "Vengeance is mine, I will repay, says the Lord." No, "if your enemies are hungry, feed them; if they are thirsty, give them something to drink; for by doing this you will heap burning coals on their heads." Do not be overcome by evil, but overcome evil with good. (Romans 12:9–21)

Paul's words are not only an articulate paraphrase of Jesus' moral teachings; they also show how the principles of the great commandments, the Beatitudes, and the Golden Rule can be applied in daily life.

After we confess the Apostles' Creed, let us read what Matthew, Mark, and Luke have to say about Jesus' words and deeds. "You will know them by their fruits," says Jesus (Matthew 7:16; Luke 6:44). Proper faith results in proper works. When our faith and trust are properly directed, then we realize that "the only thing that counts is faith working through love" (Galatians 5:6).

7

<hr/>

He Descended...
Rose...Ascended...
Will Come to Judge

NO SERIOUS PERSON TODAY doubts that Jesus of Nazareth was executed by Pontius Pilate. But what happened next? The creed asserts that Jesus was exalted by God and taken into the divine presence.

Descent to the Dead

The Old Roman Creed did not include the clause sometimes translated, "He descended into hell." These words were added at some point between the fourth and the sixth centuries. But what does it mean? The Latin terms *ad inferos* or *ad inferna* mean "the regions below," "the infernal regions"—a translation of the Greek *Hades*, which is not "hell" but the realm of the dead, a place of shadows and shades, like the Old Testament *Sheol*. Thus the original meaning of these words in the Apostles' Creed is simply that Jesus died—he went to the place where the dead go, and we should translate simply, "He descended to the dead."

Medieval theologians, however, began to link these words with the statement in 1 Peter 3:18–20, that Jesus "was put to death in the flesh, but made alive in the spirit, in which also he went and made a proclamation to the spirits in prison, who in former times did not obey, when God waited patiently in the days of Noah. . . ." The same writer, in 4:6, repeats his assertion that "the gospel was proclaimed even to the dead." These passages, however, do not say that Jesus preached "to the spirits in prison" in the interval between his death and resurrection, and some interpreters believe that the writer asserts that Jesus preached to the spirits of the other world *after* the resurrection. In any case, 1 Peter reflects awareness of the problem of explaining the eternal fate of those who died before they had heard the gospel.

By the time of the Reformation, in the sixteenth century, theologians generally interpreted *inferna* as "hell," the eternal abode of the damned, but they explained this in opposite ways. John Calvin believed that Jesus' soul—not his body, which lay in the tomb—descended into hell to share the worst terrors of the damned. Early Lutherans, however, following Martin Luther, believed that Jesus descended into hell in both body and soul after his burial. There he "conquered the devil, destroyed the power of hell, and took from the devil all his power" so that "neither hell nor the devil can capture or harm us and all who believe in Christ" (Article 9, Solid Declaration, Formula of Concord, 1577 A.D.).

"He descended to the dead," therefore, is the fifth phrase in the series that is intended to exclude the Gnostic theory that Jesus somehow did not die as all other humans die. He (1) suffered under Pontius Pilate, (2) was crucified, (3) died, (4) was buried, and (5) descended to the dead.

On the Third Day He Rose Again

The earliest Christians believed that God had exalted Jesus after his death and taken him into the divine presence, but they struggled to understand and explain this. Although there is in the New Testament no description of what happened to Jesus during the actual resurrection, these believers have left us two kinds of evidence that support their conviction that Jesus was exalted by God. There are narratives of the discovery of the empty tomb and there are also reports of the risen Jesus' appearances to believers.

The discovery of the empty tomb is reported in all four Gospels, with curious differences of detail (Mark 16:1–8; Matthew 28:1–10; Luke 24:1–11; John 20:1–10). They agree that it was Mary Magdalene who first came to the empty tomb, but Matthew, Mark, and Luke assert that one or more other women accompanied her. They disagree whether the women came to the tomb just before dawn (John) or just after (Mark). Whom did the women see at the tomb? Mark says: "a young man"; Matthew: "an angel of the Lord"; Luke: "two men"; John: "two angels." The strangest curiosity is the report of how the women responded to their discovery. Mark, in what apparently are the last words of his Gospel, makes the astounding statement that "They said nothing to anyone, for they were afraid" (16:8). The other Gospels report that they quickly announced their joyous discovery to the male disciples.

The Christian belief in the exaltation of Jesus by God is not identical with belief in the empty tomb. The empty tomb leads only to a negative conclusion: the body of Jesus was not there. In itself it does not and cannot suggest to us what happened to Jesus.

Reports of the appearances of the risen Jesus are a more positive kind of evidence. To accept the veracity of these reports is to believe that God exalted Jesus after his death. Such appearances are reported by Matthew, Luke, John, and Paul. Luke names Cleopas and his companion as the first to see the risen Christ (Luke 24:13–35), while in John it is Mary Magdalene (John 20:14). There are differing conceptions of the risen body. Although in Luke 24:13–53 and John 20:19 Jesus appears and disappears at will, Luke also reports that the risen Jesus ate broiled fish (Luke 24:43) and had "flesh and bones" (Luke 24:39), and John invites doubting Thomas to feel the wounds in his body. Paul, however, insists that "flesh and blood cannot inherit the kingdom of God" (1 Corinthians 15:50), that what is involved is a "spiritual body" (1 Corinthians 15:44), and that the risen Jesus will change the bodies of the believers to be like his glorified body (1 Corinthians 15:49–55).

The oldest and most detailed list of witnesses of such appearances is that of Paul in 1 Corinthians 15:3–11. Paul apparently intended the items in his list to be read as occurring in sequence, from first to last:

- Cephas (the Aramaic name for the Greek translation "Peter"; both mean "rock")
- the Twelve
- more than five hundred persons at one time, "most of whom are still alive"
- James, Jesus' brother, not one of the Twelve

- "all the apostles"
- Paul

This list, which Paul says was transmitted to him—possibly at the time he joined the believers—might be composed of two originally separate lists of three items each. There is a balance between Peter and James, between the Twelve and "all the apostles," and the irregular appearance to more than five hundred and to Paul. That Peter was the first witness of the resurrected Jesus is suggested also by Mark 14:28 and 16:7, and appearances to the eleven disciples are reported also in Matthew, Luke, and John. Paul, whose letters are the earliest documents of the Christian community, interprets his conversion as an appearance of the risen Jesus. Paul insists, moreover, that the kind of "spiritual body" (1 Corinthians 15:44) all believers would be granted in their resurrection would be identical to the glorified body of the risen Jesus.

The witness of the New Testament, therefore, points to three assurances of this part of the Apostles' Creed:

1. Jesus' resurrection is God's confirmation of his ministry of preaching and healing.
2. Jesus' resurrection was a transformation to a new, glorious life, free from the evils of earthy life.
3. Jesus' resurrection is the guarantee, anticipation, and "first fruits" of the resurrection of all believers.

He Ascended

"He ascended into heaven; he is seated at the right hand of the Father." Jesus' exaltation to the presence of God is explicitly asserted by several New Testament writers and presupposed by all. In John 20:17 the risen Jesus tells Mary Magdalene, "Do not hold on to me, because I have not yet ascended to the Father." Acts asserts that the risen Jesus is with God in heaven, and "standing at the right hand of God" (2:33; 3:19–21; 7:55–56). And Hebrews 1:3 proclaims that "When he had made purification for sins, he sat down at the right hand of the Majesty on high" (see also Hebrews 4:14; 12:2).

Only one New Testament writer, however, explicitly separates the ascension from the resurrection and provides a narrative to describe how Jesus was "carried up," "taken up," or "lifted up." The Gospel of Luke ends with this description (24:50–53), and its sequel, the book of Acts, begins with it (1:1–11). Near Bethany, a suburb of Jerusalem (Luke 24:50), or on the nearby Mount of Olives (Acts 1:12), Jesus gave his final instructions to the eleven, telling them to stay in Jerusalem until Pentecost, after which they would be his witnesses "to all nations" (Luke 24:47) or "to the ends of the earth" (Acts 1:8). Then, according to Luke 24:50–51, "lifting up his hands, he blessed them. While he was blessing them, he withdrew from them and was carried up into heaven." And Acts 1:9 reports, "as they were watching, he was lifted up, and a cloud took him out of their sight." The tradition that the ascension took place forty days after the resurrection is based entirely on the statement in Acts 1:3 that the risen Jesus appeared to his disciples "during forty days."

The ascension as narrated in Luke and Acts can scarcely be visualized in our imagination. (The image of Elijah ascending to heaven in a chariot of fire during a whirlwind in 2 Kings 2:11 is not much help in understanding Acts 1.) Jesus' ascension is a pictorial expression of the truth expressed by Paul and Hebrews, namely, that Jesus' resurrection was not a return to earthly life (as in the case of Lazarus in John 11) but rather a transformation to heavenly existence with God. From his session at "the right hand of the Father," the exalted Jesus intercedes for us with God (Hebrews 7:25).

Return as Judge

According to Mark, at Jesus' hearing before the council on the night before his death, the high priest asked him, "Are you the Messiah, the Son of the Blessed One?" Jesus answered, "I am; and 'you will see the Son of Man seated at the right hand of the Power' and 'coming with the clouds of heaven' " (Mark 14:61–62, an allusion to Daniel 7:13). On numerous other occasions Jesus also spoke of the Son of Man coming in the glory of God (for example, Mark 8:38; Matthew 16:27; Luke 9:26). Moreover, he was remembered as having spoken of an imminent change in history, as in Mark 9:1, "There are some standing here who will not taste death until they see that the kingdom of God has come with power." But when the disciples begged to know the date of the end and the coming of the Son of Man on the clouds, Jesus emphatically demurred: "About that day or hour no one knows, neither the angels in heaven, nor the Son, but only the Father" (Mark 13:32). Although many readers have wondered precisely what such statements mean, the early Christians were convinced that Jesus spoke of his return to judge humankind at the end of history.

Many of the earliest believers seem to have been disappointed and confused that the return of Jesus had not occurred after the passing of a few decades. Paul included in his preaching to Gentiles a firm hope in the imminent return of Christ (1 Thessalonians 4:15–17; 1 Corinthians 15:23–24). In 1 Thessalonians 5:1–11 Paul warned his converts to be on the alert for "the day of the Lord." But he learned that his readers had become alarmed, and he found it necessary to urge them not to quit their daily work, thinking that the "day of the Lord is already here" (2 Thessalonians 2:2). The writer of James 5:7 urges his readers, "Be patient . . . until the coming of the Lord." And one of the main issues taken up by the author of 2 Peter, a late writer of the New Testament, is the "delay of the *parousia*" (Greek for "coming"). Some were "scoffing . . . saying, 'Where is the promise of his coming? . . . All things continue as they were from the beginning of creation'" (2 Peter 3:3–7). The book of Revelation, after lengthy and graphic descriptions of the events leading up to the end, includes as the final prayer, "Amen. Come, Lord Jesus!" (22:20). It is therefore not surprising that the Apostles' Creed includes the affirmation, "He will come again to judge the living and the dead."

The purpose of Jesus' return, according to the creed, is "to judge the living and the dead." The theme of divine judgment runs from Genesis through Revelation. In the Old Testament, God is "the Judge of all the earth" (Genesis 18:25), a motif that recurs again and again in the Psalms (for example, 50:1–6, 75:2, 96:10–13, 98:8–9).

In the New Testament, Paul speaks about "the day when . . . God, through Jesus Christ, will judge the secret thoughts of all" (Romans 2:16), "the day of wrath, when God's righteous judgment will be revealed . . . according to each one's deeds" (Romans 2:5–6). Salvation, however, comes as a free gift to all who believe (Romans 3:22). Most famously, Matthew, in 25:31–46, writes a narrative about the "great assize," the last judgment. The Son of Man presides on his throne, surrounded by angels. The "nations" (or "Gentiles") are gathered before him, and he separates them into two groups. One group is blessed by the Father and will inherit the kingdom prepared for them "from the foundation of the world." The others are sent into "eternal punishment." And the criterion for judgment is whether they have lived according to Jesus' teachings of compassion: feeding the hungry, giving drink to the thirsty, welcoming the stranger, clothing the naked, caring for the sick, and visiting the prisoners.

Although language about divine wrath and punishment does indeed occur in both Testaments, judgment has more to do with setting things right, creating a just order, than with wreaking vengeance. Evil is an undeniable reality in our world, and justice often goes lacking. It is only natural that we, like the biblical writers, would look forward to the time when justice prevails.

The assertions that Jesus descended to the dead, rose again, ascended, and will return as judge all describe actions that are beyond the course of earthly life. We can describe such concepts no more easily than we can picture them in our minds. They hold before us, however, not only the reality of death but also the lively hope for a transformed life after death. And the hope for the return of Jesus reminds us that evil is still a reality in our world; the kingdom of God is not fully implemented. We look forward to the unqualified elimination of evil in all its forms by God in the future.

8

———— ⋅◦⋅ ————

I Believe in the Holy Spirit

CHRISTIANS OFTEN HAVE DIFFICULTY thinking in concrete terms about the Holy Spirit—and understandably so. It is far easier to gain a mental image of Jesus, an actual man in history who lived in a specific time and place. Jesus' actions and teachings can be approached by methods of historical research. And yet the Christian church during its long history has sung hymns to the Spirit, prayed to the Spirit, and confessed that the Spirit is one of three "persons" in the Holy Trinity.

The word "spirit" itself is not easy to define. We speak of someone being "in good spirits," of a "spirited animal," of "school spirit," of "the spirit of the times," and of "the spirit world." But who or what is the "Holy Spirit"? In both of the major languages in which the Bible was originally written, the word for "spirit" also means "wind" or "breath" (Hebrew *ruah*, and Greek *pneuma*).

Thus there are double meanings in some biblical texts, for example, John 3:8, "The wind-Spirit blows where it chooses." Your "spirit" is the "breath" of life that enables you to be active. God's Spirit is God's activity throughout all the ages, beginning with the creation of the world and continuing into our lives today.

God's Spirit in the Bible

In both Old and New Testaments, God's activity in relation to the world is presented as the activity of the Holy Spirit. This begins with the creation, when "a wind [*ruah*] from God swept over the face of the waters" (Genesis 1:2). This wind that whipped up waves in the total darkness of the chaotic primeval ocean was God's breath, God's Spirit, beginning the process of creation. The Spirit continued to be active in inspiring the prophets. Ezekiel proclaimed that the Spirit could bring life to the dead: "I will put my spirit within you, and you shall live . . . I the Lord have spoken and will act" (37:14). And the prophet Joel looked to the distant future when God "will pour out my [God's] spirit on all flesh; your sons and your daughters shall prophesy, your old men shall dream dreams, and your young men shall see visions" (2:28; Acts 2 finds the fulfillment of this passage to be the descent of the Spirit on the early believers on the day of Pentecost).

According to the Gospels, the Spirit of God began to direct Jesus' actions from the time of his baptism by John (Mark 1:10; Matthew 3:16; Luke 3:22). And Luke reports that Jesus, in his first sermon, in his hometown of Nazareth, quoted Isaiah 61:1–2,

> The Spirit of the Lord is upon me,
>> because he has anointed me to bring good news to the
> poor.

He has sent me to proclaim release to the captives
and recovery of sight to the blind,
to let the oppressed go free,
to proclaim the year of the Lord's favor. (Luke 4:18–19)

John 20:22 asserts that, on the evening of the day of resurrection, the risen Jesus "breathed on them and said to them, 'Receive the Holy Spirit'" (this is John's version of the Pentecost experience, which Acts 2:1–4 dates to seven weeks later). Paul repeatedly reminded his converts that they had received the Holy Spirit. Romans 5:5 asserts, "God's love has been poured into our hearts through the Holy Spirit that has been given to us." The believer, therefore, will "walk not according to the flesh but according to the Spirit . . . since the Spirit of God dwells in you" (Romans 8:4, 9). "Do you not know that you are God's temple and that God's Spirit dwells in you?" (1 Corinthians 3:16).

The Gospel of John has distinctive terms for the Holy Spirit and for the Spirit's activity. The Spirit is the *Paraclete*, that is, the counselor, helper, advocate, and defense attorney (John 14:16, 26; 15:26; 16:7) who functions to defend us from evil. The Spirit is also the "Spirit of truth" (John 14:17, 16:13) who—in a strange statement—will continue to reveal things to the believers after Jesus' departure (John 16:12–15). The Spirit takes over some of the functions that Jesus filled during his ministry.

The Third Person

The Holy Spirit, according to orthodox Christian thought, is the third "person" of the Trinity. The Apostles' Creed says nothing on this matter other than that we believe in the Spirit. The Nicene Creed, however, adds several phrases:

> We believe in the Holy Spirit, the Lord, the giver of life,
>   who proceeds from the Father [and the Son],
>   who with the Father and the Son is worshiped and
>   glorified,
>   who has spoken through the prophets.

In view of the fact that the New Testament uniformly calls Jesus "Lord" (*kyrios*), it is remarkable that the Nicene Creed applied this title to the Spirit. That the Spirit inspires the prophets and gives life is a common theme in the Old Testament (see the comment on Ezekiel 37:14, above). A difference between the Eastern and the Western churches emerged when the Western church in the sixth century added the phrase "and the Son" (the *filioque* phrase) to the creed, asserting that the Spirit proceeds from the Father "*and the Son.*" The original Nicene Creed simply stated that the Spirit "proceeds from the Father," a conviction held yet today by all Eastern Orthodox Christians. Most Christians, however, would agree that the significance of this dispute might not be worth the hours of weighty discussion and the quarts of spilled ink spent on it over the centuries.

Gifts of the Spirit

In the earliest period of the Israelite occupation of Canaan, we read of persons—both Israelites and Canaanites—who experienced being literally "spirit possessed." At the time of the judges, "The spirit of the LORD took possession of Gideon," stimulating him to lead a battle (Judges 6:34). Other judges—Othniel (Judges 3:10), Jephthah (Judges 11:29), and Samson (Judges 13:25, 14:6, 15:14)—were similarly possessed. Soon after Samuel anointed Saul as the first king of Israel, he met "a band of prophets . . . and the spirit of God possessed him, and he fell into a prophetic frenzy along with them" (1 Samuel 10:10). At a later time, Saul had a similar experience: "The spirit of God came upon him. As he was going, he fell into a prophetic frenzy. . . . He too stripped off his clothes, and he too fell into a frenzy before Samuel" (1 Samuel 19:23–24). Among the prophets, it is especially Ezekiel who has such charismatic experiences. He reports, "The spirit entered into me" (Ezekiel 3:24), and "The spirit of the LORD fell upon me" and caused him to prophesy (11:5).

There are echoes of such experiences also in the New Testament. The book of Acts frequently refers to persons being "filled with the Holy Spirit" (for example, 2:4, 4:8, 6:3, 9:17, 13:52) and of the Holy Spirit "falling" on believers (for example, 1:8, 8:14–17, 10:44, 11:15, 19:6). The precise nature of this experience is the subject of debate among various Christian denominations.

Paul is more specific about the workings of the Spirit of God in the lives of the believers. The Spirit produces the specific "fruit" of "love, joy, peace, patience, kindness, generosity, faithfulness, gentleness, and self-control" (Galatians 5:22–23). The Spirit, moreover, ignites in individual believers various gifts, talents, and proficiencies that benefit the entire community (1 Corinthians 12). The New Testament word for these "gifts" is *charismata* (the singular form is *charisma*), a word that is closely related to the Greek word for "grace," *charis*. This suggests that behind the idea of the "gifts of the Spirit" lies the conviction that God's grace kindles within our hearts various graces or powers. Paul lists nine charismata in 1 Corinthians 12:8–10: wisdom, knowledge, faith, healing, miracles, prophecy, discernment of spirits, tongues, and the interpretation of tongues. In the next chapter, however, Paul puts three spiritual gifts above all else: faith, hope, and love (1 Corinthians 13:13). Of all the gifts, only love is permanent; it alone will endure into the next life.

The gifts of the Spirit are the subject of 1 Corinthians 12–14. Paul apparently wrote this section in response to the Corinthians' question whether they should allow in their worship services the practice of speaking in tongues (*glossolalia*). Paul suggested that, with proper supervision and qualifications, this could be allowed, but that the higher gifts should be most sought—and especially the greatest of all charismata, namely, love.

Members of the modern Pentecostal movement generally hold that gifts of the Spirit are given to the Christian subsequent to water baptism, when the Christian has a spiritual experience of the Holy Spirit that is sometimes called "baptism in the Holy Spirit" or the "baptism of the Spirit," "the second baptism," or "rebirth in the Spirit." Churches of the Reformation, along with Roman Catholics and Eastern Orthodox Christians, however, believe that the Holy Spirit comes to the individual at the time of water baptism. The only place in the New Testament where the reception of the Holy Spirit is separated from water baptism is the strange story in Acts 8:14–17, where something about the water baptism seems to have been problematic. And according to a noteworthy narrative in Acts 19:1–7, Apollos, a Christian missionary from Alexandria, was baptizing his converts "into John's baptism," which was a "baptism of repentance" (verse 4). These converts had not "received the Holy Spirit" at that baptism. Paul therefore baptized them "in the name of the Lord Jesus" (verse 5), at which time the Spirit was then communicated to them (verse 6). This indicates that the writer of Acts and also (presumably) Paul expected that converts received the Spirit at the time of water baptism.

God has given each person worthy gifts and talents. These gifts differ from person to person, but all come from the same source, and all are given for the common good. "There are varieties of gifts, but the same Spirit . . . and there are varieties of activities, but it is the same God who activates all of them in everyone. To each is given the manifestation of the Spirit for the common good" (1 Corinthians 12:4–7).

9

––––––⊷◦⊷––––––

I Believe in the
Holy Catholic Church,
the Communion of Saints

IS IT NOT STRANGE that the creed calls us to believe in *the church*? Is it not enough that we believe in God the Father, his only Son, and the Holy Spirit? If we imagine the situation of the Christian believers somewhere around 200 A.D., when the Old Roman Creed affirmed belief in "the holy church," this part of the Apostles' Creed will be more understandable. Christians in the first three centuries were markedly set off from the majority culture, and persecution from Roman officials could have broken out at any time. The larger community viewed the Christians as "atheists" who denied the traditional gods, as unpatriotic parasites who rejected service to the state, and as a threat to the stability of society because of their egalitarian views. To believe in the church in that situation was a most serious confession. It was to affirm that in the circle of those who believed in Jesus you found your orientation to this life and your hope for the life to come.

The Church on Earth: Exclusive or Inclusive?

The word "church" has multiple meanings. It can refer to a building, to a denomination, and to a local congregation. When we say in the creed that we believe in the church, however, we are referring to a more abstract concept, one that is not easy to define. Broadly speaking, the church consists of all the people of God from all times and places. Speaking more narrowly, the church is a gathering of people in congregations who trust in God through the work and intercession of Jesus Christ.

The most common term for the church in the original Greek of the New Testament is *ekklesia*, from *ek*, "out of," and *kaleo*, "I call." (*Ekklesia* occurs only twice in the Gospels—Matthew 16:18 and 18:17—but it is frequently used in Acts and the letters.) The church consists of those "called out" of the world and called to gather together in fellowship. Theologians therefore refer to discussion about the nature of the church as "ecclesiology."

Many issues about the nature of the church have been debated throughout the centuries. In the Apostles' Creed, the expression "communion of saints" defines the phrase "the holy catholic Church." The church is the communion of saints. "Saints" here refers to all Christians. "The communion of saints," therefore, can be translated as "the fellowship of believers." Both expressions presuppose the concept of the church as a pure society, a community of sincere believers. This view of the church on earth is sometimes called the "exclusive" view, as opposed to the "inclusive" view—that the church on earth consists both of believers and unbelievers, saints and sinners, faithful and hypocrites alike, and that God in the final judgment will separate the good from the bad. Jesus' parable of the wheat and the weeds in Matthew 13:24–30 is often interpreted as referring to the church on earth. Should the farmer pull the weeds out of the wheat field? No, says Jesus, for "the weeds would uproot the wheat along with them. Let both of them grow together until the harvest," when the weeds would be burned and the wheat gathered into the barn.

Early Christians had strong debates on the question of the purity of the church. Some bishops argued that the church, as the communion of saints, was a holy community that could not tolerate impurity in its midst. If a church member denied Christ during persecution, there would be no chance for him or her to be readmitted. There could be no "second repentance." The more inclusive view finally prevailed, however, when bishops in the third century A.D. argued that the church was like Noah's ark, which contained both clean and unclean animals. (Certain wags today say that the church is like Noah's ark in another sense: you can stand the stench inside only because of the deluge outside!) If the church excludes someone from its fellowship, that person is cut off from the institution that proclaims the gospel. So, today the inclusive view of the church on earth is favored by the great majority of Christians, while smaller groups like the Amish, strict Mennonites, and others attempt to maintain the exclusive view.

In an ideal sense, however, the purist ideal is retained by most Christian groups in the concept of the "one holy church." The church is "militant" on earth, warring against evil, but in the future it will be "triumphant," victorious over all that hampers authentic life. The church is "visible" in the form of earthly institutions, but since it consists of all believers from all places and all times, including those who have died and those who are yet to be born, it is "invisible." The distinction between "the church" and "the churches" is significant.

The contrast between the church and the churches is made evident by the many different church structures on earth—Lutheran, Roman Catholic, Methodist, Episcopalian, Eastern Orthodox, Baptists, and many others. The splintering of the church on earth is due to disagreements over the meaning of certain teachings and also, in part, to the different forms that Christianity took when it reached different parts of the world. But there is ultimately only one church; it consists of those who have been, are being, and will be redeemed through God's grace.

The Origin of the Church

When did the church begin? This question has been much discussed, and there are many cogent answers. The church can be said to have originated in eternity, in the mind of God. But, thinking more historically, some have argued that it began at the moment of Jesus' birth—the incarnation of God. Others locate the origin of the church at the baptism of Jesus, which marked the beginning of his ministry. Or should we trace its origin to Jesus' call of the disciples, the nucleus of the future church? Perhaps it began at the Last Supper, when Jesus invited his disciples to continue their fellowship after his death. The most widespread view is that the church began on the Day of Pentecost as described in the second chapter of Acts. A more accurate reading of Acts 2, however, reveals that that narrative describes not the birth of the church but the beginning of its outreach, its universal mission.

Another answer is possible when we observe the specific belief that distinguishes Christians from others. Everyone believes that Jesus was born, that he was baptized, that he engaged in preaching and healing, and that he died. Everyone also believes that his followers gradually developed a new religion that came to be dominant in the Roman Empire. But can anyone believe in the resurrection and not be a Christian believer? The Christian church began when those persons who had followed Jesus during his ministry came to believe in his resurrection and gathered together into a fellowship. This happened in Jerusalem in 30 A.D. Both historically and theologically, therefore, it is most accurate to say that the birth of the Christian church coincides with the emergence of the resurrection faith.

Images and Marks of the Church

Already in the New Testament we find a variety of honorific terms for the believers as a community. They are the "flock" over which the Holy Spirit has appointed overseers (Acts 20:28); "God's field, God's building" (1 Corinthians 3:9); "the temple of the living God" (2 Corinthians 6:16); "the family of faith" (Galatians 6:10); "citizens with the saints and also members of the household of God" (Ephesians 2:19); and "the household of God, which is the church of the living God, the pillar and bulwark of the truth" (1 Timothy 3:15). The description in 1 Peter 2:9—"a chosen race, a royal priesthood, a holy nation, God's own people"—applies the prerogatives and privileges given to Israel in the Old Testament to the church.

One of the most memorable images of the church goes back to Paul, who spoke of the believers and members of the "body of Christ." There has been much speculation about the origin of this thought—whether it reflects the Old Testament concept of "corporate personality" or certain mystical strains in Judaism. But it is strangely reminiscent of the story in Acts 9:1–9 of Paul's "conversion," when he was blinded by a "light from heaven" and heard a voice saying, "Saul, Saul, why do you persecute me?" Paul (the Roman name; Saul is the Hebrew name) responded, "Who are you, Lord?" The answer: "I am Jesus, whom you are persecuting." In persecuting the believers, Paul was persecuting the church. This conversation therefore presupposes a shared identity between the risen Jesus and the community of believers.

In any case, Paul speaks of the Lord's Supper as a "sharing in the body of Christ," which makes the "many" into "one body" (1 Corinthians 10:16–17). His most extensive development of this theme is in 1 Corinthians 12:3–31, where he states explicitly, "You are the body of Christ and individually members of it" (verse 27). Membership in this body begins with baptism (verse 13), at which time the Holy Spirit ignites distinctive "gifts" to each believer. Differences among the community must be respected, and each individual's contribution should be respected. That all belong to one body also suggests that the individual members should acknowledge their connection to other believers and to Jesus. The idea of church as the body of Christ is taken up in Colossians 1:18, 24 ("He is the head of the body, the church"); and Ephesians 1:22–23; 4:12; 5:23, 30.

The Apostles' Creed describes the church as "holy" and as "the communion of saints." The Nicene Creed, especially as revised in the latter part of the fourth century, formulates the traditional "marks of the church." It is one, holy, catholic, and apostolic. Some of these marks are found already in the New Testament, and all are familiar from Christian writings of the second century. These marks are idealistic when we consider the actual congregations on earth, but they are realistic when applied to the invisible totality of the people of God or to the triumphant church of the future. The *oneness* of the church is communicated especially in the image of the body of Christ. The *holiness* of the church refers to the work of the Holy Spirit in its midst, as well as to the holiness granted to its members by the grace of God. The church is *catholic*, which means universal—an alternate way of referring to its unity. And the church is *apostolic* in the sense that it reveres the apostolic writings (the New Testament), the apostolic teachings (the Apostles' Creed), and apostolic authority (as the bishops gradually came to be considered the successors of the apostles).

There always has been and probably always will be a tension between the church as institution and the church as the totality of believers. Already in the third century, bishop Cyprian of North Africa viewed the church as an earthly institution identifiable by the proper succession of bishops from the apostles. He contended that "outside of the church there is no salvation." Anyone not related to the true church, governed by the true succession from the apostles, is excluded from salvation. If, however, the one true church consists of all persons of all times and places who receive God's grace through Jesus Christ, then, by definition, it is true that outside the church there is no salvation—with no requirement of belonging to any one earthly institution, however venerable it might be. Recall that, according to Luke, the repentant thief who was crucified with Jesus had no chance of joining any Christian denomination but was nonetheless invited by Jesus to paradise (Luke 23:40–43).

10

I Believe in the
Forgiveness of Sins

THE CREED EMPHASIZES Jesus' death in order to exclude those
who denied the reality of Jesus' human body—for example, the
Gnostics—but it does so also for another reason, a reason that has
been significant for most Christian believers of all ages. According to all early Christian writings, Jesus' death was not only a
historical fact; it was a redemptive event. He died *for us*. When
Paul joined the Christian believers, he was taught—among other
things—that "Christ died for our sins" (1 Corinthians 15:3). The
Gospels also uniformly assert that Jesus' death was an act of God
for the salvation of humankind. Mark attributes such thoughts to
Jesus himself: "The Son of Man came not to be served but to serve,
and to give his life a ransom for many" (Mark 10:45; also Matthew
20:28). John has distinctive language for a similar thought: "Just

as Moses lifted up the serpent in the wilderness, so must the Son of Man be lifted up, that whoever believes in him may have eternal life" (John 3:14–15). Christians have spent countless hours and have written hundreds of books in the attempt to understand how Jesus' death could lead to redemption for those who believe in him. What did it mean that the earliest believers said that Jesus died for them, and what can it mean for us? In what way could Jesus' death bring salvation to the human race?

How Did We Go Wrong?

Few Christians would agree with Voltaire's Candide that "All is for the best in this, the best of all possible worlds." Both the Old Testament and the New Testament are clear that human sinfulness is universal. "There is no one who does good, no, not one," says the psalmist (Psalm 14:3). And Jeremiah complains, "The heart is devious above all else; it is perverse—who can understand it?" (Jeremiah 17:9). Paul cites such verses in Romans 3:10–18 and then concludes that "all have sinned and fall short of the glory of God" (Romans 3:23). Christians, however, have often debated about the cause of the "fallenness" of creation. Are human beings perfectible? Are they able not to sin? Are sin and guilt inherited? Is there such a thing as "original sin," and if so, what is it? If humans had not sinned at the beginning, would we not die? What is the relation between the story of the sin of Adam and Eve in the Garden of Eden and our sin?

Two opposing views on these questions emerged in a heated debate around 400 A.D., in the controversy between Augustine, bishop of Hippo in North Africa, and the British monk Pelagius. Augustine, arguing from his own youthful moral struggles, held that the sin of Adam and Eve resulted in the permanent corruption of their nature. All persons subsequently born came into this world with guilt inherited from the first human couple and also with the tendency to commit sin. In addition, according to Augustine, the sin of Adam and Eve resulted in death; if they had not sinned, they would not have died. Augustine believed that the guilt of this "original sin" was removed by baptism, while the struggle against the tendency to commit sin is lifelong.

Pelagius seems to have taught that each person is born into this world in the same condition as that in which Adam and Eve were created. The essence of this human nature was—and still is, according to Pelagius—free will. It always was, is now, and always will be possible not to sin. Sin is the result of human will. Therefore the sin of Adam and Eve, resulting from misuse of free will, is similar to the sin of all subsequent human beings. And yet, according to Pelagius, God does not force us to sin, much less impute to us the consequences of the sin of our ancestors. The concept of original sin appeared to Pelagius to be a denial of God's justice and goodness. Pelagius believed that humans were created mortal; Adam and Eve would have died even if they had not sinned.

In general, the Protestant Reformers, and especially Martin Luther and John Calvin, took the side of Augustine in this controversy. Luther strongly emphasized that the entire hope for human salvation lies in the grace of God rather than in what we humans can do. Sin, according to Luther, is not merely a collection of wrong acts; it is the condition of being unable not to sin. Sins, moreover, may be those of commission (wrongful acts, thoughts, or words) or of omission (neglected duties and responsibilities); both are equally serious.

Sin and Its Results

If sin is a universal human condition, then it is not surprising to find in the Bible a variety of terms that attempt to express this reality. *Transgression* refers to the breaking of commandments, a concept that is closely connected with the Law of Moses. So Galatians 3:19 says, "Why then the law? It was added because of transgressions." And Romans 4:15, "Where there is no law there is no transgression" (RSV). *Iniquity*, a common term in the Psalms (for example, 32:5, 40:12, 90:8), occurs also in Hebrews 8:12, Romans 4:7, and in other places. The term conveys the idea of lawlessness or gross lack of justice. *Trespass* is a lapse, fall, or failure. Paul refers to the sin of Adam and Eve in the Garden of Eden as a trespass (Romans 5:12–21), and he is sure that Jesus "was handed over to death for our trespasses (Romans 4:25). The term *sin* is a general and frequent term in both Testaments for missing the mark, going wrong, or falling short of the life God intended; Paul uses this word forty-eight times in his New Testament letters.

Evil brings suffering, whether it is found in the natural world or within the human heart. Sin results in human misery, even when the sinner might be forgiven. For example, a murderer may be forgiven, but the effects of the sinful act remain for those who knew the victim. The New Testament asserts that "the wages of sin is death" (Romans 6:23). Theologians have sometimes taught that this includes both physical death and spiritual death (separation from God). In any case, the results of sin are predictable and automatic. It is impossible to sin without causing suffering to the victim as well as to the sinner. This does not mean that God sends the suffering; it is the automatic by-product of sin. God's "wrath" denotes God's natural displeasure at the vicious cycle of evil rather than a feeling of "vengeance."

Paul distinctively likens our experience of sin with the condition of slavery (Galatians 4:3; Romans 6:16, 8:15). It is something from which we cannot free ourselves—a kind of addiction, the inability to see our desperate need for deliverance, in which hope comes only when we acknowledge our helplessness. The beginning of redemption occurs when we utter the cry, "Wretched man that I am! Who will rescue me from this body of death?" (Romans 7:24). The answer: "Thanks be to God through Jesus Christ our Lord!" (Romans 7:25).

Metaphors for Salvation

The New Testament uses a number of terms to suggest the effects of Jesus' death on human salvation, each of which has a distinctive thrust.

- *Salvation* is a general term; it refers to deliverance and rescue: "You are to call his name Jesus, for he will save his people from their sins" (Matthew 1:21).
- The word *redemption* was used in Jesus' time to refer to the purchase of freedom for slaves—or the slave purchasing his or her own freedom. Thus Paul refers to Christians as slaves who have been freed—redeemed—from slavery to sin and death (Galatians 4:1–7; Romans 6:16, 8:2).
- Former slaves, says Paul, now have the status of adopted children of God, stepsiblings of Jesus and heirs with him of God's blessings (Galatians 4:3–7; Romans 8:14–17). *Adoption* was a common practice among Greeks and Romans, but rare among Jews. Under Roman law, an adopted child had rights equal to those of natural-born

children. The term "adoption" occurs in the Bible only in the Pauline writings of the New Testament.

- The word *forgiveness* comes from the area of personal relationships. Its Greek form (*aphiemi*) means to "let go," that is, to refuse to hang on to hurts or insults that prevent the enjoyment of life. "Forgiveness" is often related to "repentance." A person repents, and the offended one forgives. It is striking—and important—that Paul seldom speaks either of repentance (only Romans 2:4 and 2 Corinthians 7:9 and 12:21) or of forgiveness (only in the "deutero-Pauline" parallel verses, Ephesians 1:7 and Colossians 1:14). These terms do not fit Paul's view of sin as the condition of slavery; a slave needs deliverance, not necessarily forgiveness. Moreover, forgiveness implies a change of God's attitude; Paul insists that God takes the initiative in human salvation. The problem lies with human beings, not with God.

- Some early Christians viewed the death of Jesus as God's way to *reconcile* the estranged world to himself: "In Christ God was reconciling the world to himself" (2 Corinthians 5:19; also Romans 5:10).

- In view of the Israelite practice of the sacrifice of animals for atonement for sins, it is not surprising that some Christians thought of Jesus' death as the ultimate *sacrifice* for sin: "Christ . . . offered for all time a single sacrifice for sins" (Hebrews 10:12).

- Paul speaks of the death of Jesus as the means by which God *justifies* the sinner, which is to pronounce a "not guilty" verdict. *Justification* is a legal metaphor that has a place in the court of justice. The most striking—even shocking—statement Paul makes is that God "justifies

the ungodly" (Romans 4:5), that is, pronounces the
ungodly to be not guilty. Although we might wonder
whether this is a just verdict, it shows how Paul puts
the entire initiative for human salvation in the hands
of God.

Whether we speak of redemption, adoption, forgiveness, rec-
onciliation, or justification, we are pointing to the same reality—
the experience of God's steadfast love for humankind.

Although the New Testament repeatedly asserts that human
salvation is wrought by the death of Jesus, it nowhere gives a
simple explanation of how this happens. As a result, throughout church history there have been several "atonement theories,"
none of which has been officially and exclusively adopted as
"dogma." These theories include the ideas of ransom, a cosmic
battle, satisfaction (as in medieval times), the example of divine
love, and sacrifice for sin.

1. Mark referred to Jesus' death as a *ransom* (see above). Some
later Christians, notably the biblical scholar Origen of Alexandria
(who died about 254 A.D. after being persecuted), speculated that
because of sin, the human race had fallen under the domination
of the devil. Jesus' death was the ransom paid to purchase human
freedom. Some Christians added that the devil was duped by
God: thinking that death would put an end to Christ, the devil
was surprised at God raising Jesus from death. (The analogy of
the human flesh of Jesus as bait on a fishhook was used by Martin
Luther at times.) But how can we think that God owed the devil
anything, much less the life of Jesus?

2. Others elaborated on the idea of Jesus' death as a cosmic
battle against the powers of evil, as suggested in Colossians 2:15:
In the cross, Jesus "disarmed the rulers and authorities and made

a public example of them, triumphing over them in it." Although Jesus most certainly struggled against the principalities and powers of the world, it is difficult to explain precisely how we can conceptualize such a battle except in mythological terms. We can, however, view the cross as the sign that points to the ultimate vanquishing of all forces of evil.

3. The medieval theologian Anselm of Canterbury (1033–1109) interpreted the effects of Jesus' death in terms of the feudal idea of "satisfaction," as when a master was insulted by an inferior and the offense needed to be balanced or "satisfied." Sin, as offense against the infinite God, requires infinite satisfaction. No human can offer anything infinite. Therefore God had to become human. Jesus, living a perfect human life, died to "satisfy" the infinite offense of human sin. But, we automatically ask, does God operate in terms of a medieval feudal system? Can we really believe in the pettiness of God?

4. Anselm's near contemporary, Peter Abelard (1079–1142), suggested that Jesus' death was the supreme example of God's love, which was intended to produce in us a similar love: "We love because he first loved us" (1 John 4:19). Adherents of such a view of atonement often speak of God sending Jesus to suffer and die in our place: "God so loved the world that he gave his only Son" (John 3:16). Critics of this approach, however, contend that to think of God sending Jesus to the cross as a moral lesson for us is to attribute to God a form of child abuse.

5. The idea of Jesus' death as the final sacrifice, bringing all forms of animal sacrifice to an end, is often combined with other theories. Historians, however, are not at all certain why ancient peoples believed that God demanded animal sacrifice.

We might never have a satisfactory explanation of precisely *how* the work of Jesus saves us, but we trust in the reality of salvation. In his Small Catechism, Martin Luther asserted that Jesus has redeemed and freed us so that "[We might] be his own, live under him in his kingdom, and serve him in everlasting righteousness, innocence, and blessedness." When we are freed from all that limits us from truly living, we share in the victory over sin and death that Jesus gained at his resurrection.

11

<hr>

I Believe in the Resurrection
and the Life Everlasting

THE APOSTLES' CREED begins with creation and ends with
our hope of resurrection to eternal life. The beginning of our life
on earth and the end of this life are matters beyond our control.
None of us chose to be born, and none of us can avoid death. The
end of earthly life, therefore, faces each of us with a question and
a challenge. How shall we understand our own death? And how
shall we live with hope in the face of our future death?

There is a tinge of sadness just below the surface of human
existence, even though it is often unspoken or even unrecog-
nized. This sadness comes from the thought that everything that
lives in the natural world is transitory, including our fragile and
brief lives. Stephen Foster (1826–1864) captured this melancholy
in a memorable song:

Sad is my heart for the blighted plants—
   Its pleasures are aye as brief—
They bloom at the young year's joyful call,
   And fade with the autumn leaf.
Ah! may the red rose live always,
   To smile upon earth and sky!
Why should the beautiful ever weep?
   Why should the beautiful die?

However much we try to mask the experience of death, it retains its terror for us and, when the end draws near, we cannot but think of how short our lives are. The brevity and difficulty of life are common themes in Old Testament poetry. The anonymous poet of Isaiah 40:6–8 laments,

All people are grass,
   their constancy is like the flower of the field.
The grass withers, the flower fades,
   when the breath of the LORD blows upon it;
   surely the people are grass.
The grass withers, the flower fades;
   but the word of our God will stand forever.

Job complains,

My days are swifter than a weaver's shuttle,
   and come to their end without hope.
                    (Job 7:6)

And the psalmist is at a low point:

LORD, let me know my end,
   and what is the measure of my days;
   let me know how fleeting my life is.

> You have made my days a few handbreadths,
>   and my lifetime is as nothing in your sight.
> Surely everyone stands as a mere breath.
> Surely everyone goes about like a shadow.
> Surely for nothing they are in turmoil;
>   they heap up, and do not know who will gather.
>
>   (Psalm 39:4–6)

Ancient Israelites had vague conceptions of what happens at death. The abode of the dead is *Sheol* (Greek *Hades*; Latin *inferna*), a place of forgetfulness, of shadows, of not-knowing, of the inability to praise God. "There is no work or thought or knowledge or wisdom in Sheol, to which you are going" (Ecclesiastes 9:10).

> The eye that beholds me will see me no more;
>   while your eyes are upon me, I shall be gone.
> As the cloud fades and vanishes,
>   so those who go down to Sheol do not come up;
> they return no more to their houses,
>   nor do their places know them any more.
>
>   (Job 7:8–10)

> Do you work wonders for the dead?
>   Do the shades rise up to praise you?
> Is your steadfast love declared in the grave,
>   or your faithfulness in Abaddon?
> Are your wonders known in the darkness,
>   or your saving help in the land of forgetfulness?
>
>   (Psalm 88:10–12)

> The dead do not praise the LORD,
>   nor do any that go down into silence.
>
>   (Psalm 115:17)

Martin Luther found one way to harmonize the conception of Sheol with the belief in the resurrection of the body. He frequently asserted his opinion that Sheol is where the soul "sleeps" between death and resurrection, a temporary state of being.

Views and Expectations

Because death is a universal human experience, almost all societies on earth have formed opinions about what happens when life ends. Some persons believe that death is simply extinction; at death we cease to exist, like the flame of a candle that is blown out. Various experiments today on the workings and structure of the brain seem to suggest that human consciousness ceases at the time of death. Those who believe that there is nothing for the individual after death often add that we live on in our children and their descendants—but we do not continue to live as the people we now are. This view is negatively cited in Isaiah 22:13, "Let us eat and drink, for tomorrow we die" (see also 1 Corinthians 15:32). There apparently were a few people in the early church who held similar views. According to 2 Timothy 2:17–18, certain men named Hymenaeus and Philetus "have swerved from the truth by claiming that the resurrection has already taken place." Precisely what this teaching involved is uncertain, although it suggests the idea that there is no resurrection subsequent to the believer's union with the death and resurrection of Jesus in baptism. Moreover, according to 2 Thessalonians 2:2, some early believers were convinced that "the day of the Lord is already here." Such thoughts might have resulted from a misunderstanding of Paul's teaching in Romans 6:1–11, where he asserts that "we have been buried with [Christ Jesus] by baptism into death, so that, just as Christ was raised from the dead by the glory of the Father, so we too might walk in newness of life" (verse 4).

A common belief among the religions of India and among some ancient Greeks is that the soul at death passes into another body—and again another until its purification is complete. This belief in reincarnation ("re-enfleshment") is also known as the "transmigration of souls" or, more technically, metempsychosis. The most famous Christian to support a version of reincarnation was the great church father Origen of Alexandria (he died about 254 A.D.). He taught that all souls were created by God before the creation of the cosmos. Some of these souls sinned greatly and were punished by becoming demons; others who sinned to a lesser degree were provided a human body and made to live on this earth, which was thus a place of purgation. This purification might continue into additional lives. Reincarnation, however, was rejected by most Christian theologians as incompatible with the belief in a final judgment and in heaven and hell. Also, there is not much support for the idea in the Bible, although the belief that Jesus was John the Baptist raised from the dead (Mark 6:14; 8:28), or that either Jesus or John the Baptist was a reappearance of Elijah (Matthew 17:10–13; Mark 9:11–13), has sometimes been considered evidence for the idea of reincarnation.

The medieval Christian church taught that there were four possibilities at death (or five, if you count two limbos). Those who died with gross, unforgiven sin go to a place of eternal punishment ("hell"). Those very few Christians who have great merit of good works and faith go directly to the presence of God. The vast majority of Christians, however, wind up in purgatory, an extension of earthly time, a place where the earthly or "temporal" punishment for sin can be worked off or "purged." Everyone in purgatory will eventually be taken into heaven. This belief emerged in the second century and was officially defined by the Roman church in the late Middle Ages. Roman Catholics until recently also spoke of "limbo," a destination for unbaptized infants and also for those who died without knowledge of salvation. Limbo was understood to be a state of natural happiness in which there is knowledge of God and love of God but without the "beatific vision" of God's perfect glory. In April 2007, however, Pope Benedict XVI approved a Vatican theological commission that qualified this belief, asserting that there are reasons to think that unbaptized infants will experience the fullness of salvation and be brought into the presence of God.

The Christian Hope according to the New Testament

Biblical writers without exception are realistic in their view of death. Paul refers to it as "the last enemy to be destroyed" (1 Corinthians 15:26). According to Hebrews 2:14–15, one of the main purposes of Jesus' death was to deliver those "who all their lives were held in slavery by the fear of death." The life-choking fear of death may not be completely removed by faith in the resurrection, but certainly much of its sting is diminished by it.

Jesus, unlike his contemporaries the Sadducees, taught that the dead shall rise (Mark 12:18–27). The basis for the Christian hope for the resurrection of the body and the life everlasting, however, is the resurrection of Jesus. Those who "have been baptized into Christ Jesus were baptized into his death" and "have been buried with him . . . so that, just as Christ was raised from the dead by the glory of the Father, so we too might walk in newness of life. For if we have been united with him in a death like his, we will certainly be united with him in a resurrection like his" (Romans 6:3–5). This will be a transformed and glorious life, the state in which the risen Christ lives: "He will transform the body of our humiliation that it may be conformed to the body of his glory" (Philippians 3:21). But what is the nature of this new life? The honest answer is that we do not know—nor does anyone else. "We are God's children now; what we will be has not yet been revealed" (1 John 3:2).

The most extensive description of Christian hope is given by Paul in 1 Corinthians 15. Paul first offers the evidence for the Christian belief in the resurrection of Jesus (verses 3–8; see chapter 7 above). He then argues that if you believe in the resurrection of Jesus, you cannot deny the possibility of the resurrection of deceased believers (verse 12). To deny the one is to deny the other. "If the dead are not raised, then Christ has not been raised. If Christ has not been raised, your faith is futile and you are still in your sins" (verses 16–17). Paul then presents his conception of the sequence of the end events:

- First is the resurrection of Jesus, the "first fruits of those who died" (verses 20, 23).
- Next is the return of Christ (verse 23).
- Then those who died in faith will be raised (verse 23).
- "Then comes the end, when he hands over the kingdom to God the Father, after he has destroyed every ruler and every authority and power" (verse 24).
- "The last enemy to be destroyed is death" (verse 26).
- Ultimately, all things, including the Son, will be subjected to God, "so that God may be all in all" (verse 28).

Two questions occupy the rest of 1 Corinthians 15. The first is the nature of the resurrected body. Paul believed that "flesh and blood cannot inherit the kingdom of God" (verse 50). The risen body thus is categorically different from the earthly body. "It is sown in dishonor, it is raised in glory. It is sown in weakness, it is raised in power. It is sown a physical body, it is raised a spiritual body" (verses 43–44). To speak of a "spiritual body" is to affirm both continuity and discontinuity: our "consciousness"—our personhood—will remain, but in the form of a glorified existence that cannot yet be imagined. Paul's language on the resurrection is necessarily rhetorical and metaphoric, but it points with certainty to a vision of the ultimate triumph of God.

The final question, one that bothered the Corinthian believers, has to do with what happens to the believers who are still alive when the dead are raised. Will they, unlike the risen dead, still have their old earthly bodies? If so, they would be at a disadvantage compared with those who had died. No, says Paul. "I will tell you a mystery! We will not all die, but we will all be changed, in a moment, in the twinkling of an eye," into the resurrection condition (verses 51–52). Those still alive will find themselves instantaneously transformed into the "spiritual body" of the risen dead. Then God's victory over death will be complete, and the sting of death will be no more (verses 54–57).

In our postmodern world, with its concentration on things that have only penultimate significance, the Christian hope for the ultimate universal reign of God and the destruction of death is a powerful comfort, especially for those who face the end of earthly life. This vision is movingly expressed in Revelation 21:3–4:

> See, the home of God is among mortals.
> He will dwell with them;

they will be his peoples,
and God himself will be with them;
he will wipe every tear from their eyes.
Death will be no more;
mourning and crying and pain will be no more,
for the first things have passed away.

For Further Reading

Barclay, William. *The Apostles' Creed for Everyman*. New York: Harper, 1967.

Berger, Peter L. *Questions of Faith: A Skeptical Affirmation of Christianity*. Oxford: Blackwell, 2004.

Chittister, Joan. *In Search of Belief*. Ligouri, Mo.: Triumph, 1999.

Cranfield, C. E. B. *The Apostles' Creed: A Faith to Live By*. Grand Rapids: Eerdmans, 1993.

Howell, James C. *The Life We Claim: The Apostles' Creed for Preaching, Teaching, and Worship*. Nashville: Abingdon, 2005.

Johnson, Luke Timothy. *Creed: What Christians Believe and Why It Matters*. New York: Doubleday, 2003.

Küng, Hans. *Credo: The Apostles' Creed Explained for Today*. Translated by John Bowden. New York: Doubleday, 1993.

Lash, Nicholas. *Believing Three Ways in One God: A Reading of the Apostles' Creed*. Notre Dame, Ind., and London: University of Notre Dame Press, 1992.

Schwarz, Hans. *What Christians Believe*. Philadelphia: Fortress Press, 1987.

Van Harn, Roger E. *Exploring and Proclaiming the Apostles' Creed*. Grand Rapids: Eerdmans, 2004.

Questions for Reflection and Discussion

Chapter 1. Why Creeds?

1. Suppose a neighbor tells you in a conversation that she is into "spirituality" but has little interest in "organized religion, with its clergy and creeds." How would you respond?
2. In what ways other than creeds can the Christian faith be maintained over the generations?
3. If you were to revise the Apostles' Creed, what would you add, delete, or rewrite (if anything)?

Chapter 2. I Believe in God, the Father Almighty, Creator of Heaven and Earth

1. Do you think that an atheist can have a good sense of morality? Why or why not?

2. What do you think leads some Christians to be hostile to the idea of Darwinian evolution?

3. How is a person's conception of God developed and formed? Why is it that some people think of God primarily as judge while others think of God's steadfast love?

4. What can you say to a faithful Christian who experiences tragedy? Can there be any meaningful answer to the old question of why bad things happen to good people?

Chapter 3. I Believe in Jesus Christ, God's Only Son, Our Lord

1. Albert Schweitzer, in his classic work, *The Quest of the Historical Jesus*, concluded that the titles applied to Jesus in the Gospels—Messiah, Son of Man, Son of God—are for us historical riddles, because much research is required to understand them. What designations and terms can convey the meaning of Jesus for us today?

2. If we believe that Jesus is "God's *only* Son," what does that suggest about the existence of truth in other religions?

3. Do you put more emphasis on the historical Jesus—his teachings and deeds—or on the presence of the risen Christ in the lives of believers? Why? What is the relation between these two emphases?

Chapter 4. He Was Conceived . . . and Born

1. Can you think of any reasons why there are different emphases among the New Testament Gospels? What might such differences tell us about their place of writing and their authors?
2. What do you think the Gospel writers wanted to communicate in the story of the divine conception of Jesus?
3. What is the relative importance of Christmas and Easter to Christian faith? How important to your personal faith are the narratives of Jesus' birth in comparison to the accounts of his ministry, his death, and his resurrection?

Chapter 5. He Suffered, Was Crucified, Died, Was Buried

1. Thomas Carlyle (1795–1881) wrote, "If Jesus Christ were to come today, people would not even crucify him. They would ask him to dinner, and hear what he had to say, and make fun of it." Jesus' teachings provoked strong response in first-century Palestine, both positive and negative. Is his teaching challenging today? How? Have the Gospels become inoffensive in our time? Why or why not?
2. According to Paul, "the message about the cross is foolishness to those who are perishing," "a stumbling block to Jews and foolishness to Gentiles" (1 Corinthians 1:18, 23). What do you think he meant by this?
3. The ancient Romans crucified thousands of people. How is Jesus' death unique?

Chapter 6. The Great Omission: Between Birth and Death

1. Philosopher Alfred North Whitehead once said, "As society is now constituted, a literal adherence to the moral precepts scattered throughout the Gospels would mean sudden death" (*Adventures in Ideas*, 1933). This seems similar to the statement attributed to President Harry Truman, "You can't run a country on the basis of the Sermon on the Mount." How would you respond to these opinions?

2. Some moral issues of our time, many of which deal with scientific advances like stem-cell research or the dangers of nuclear war, are not mentioned in the New Testament. How can Christians apply biblical principles to such issues?

3. In what ways have the teachings of Jesus changed or influenced your life?

Chapter 7. He Descended . . . Rose . . . Ascended . . . Will Come to Judge

1. How do you understand the statement that Jesus "descended to the dead"?

2. Some commentators assert that the resurrection is not a "historical" event in the strict sense of the word; they say it is beyond history—transhistorical or super-historical. What is your response?

3. Some Christians hold to the idea of an indestructible soul as well as to the resurrection of the body. Do you think these two conceptions can be harmonized? How?

4. How can believers today understand the narrative of the ascension of Jesus? Does the story in Acts 1:6–11 presuppose an ancient worldview (with heaven above the earth)?

Chapter 8. I Believe in the Holy Spirit

1. What images come to mind when you think of the Holy Spirit?
2. How should we consider the relation between church structures and the work of the Spirit? What happens when Christian denominations go too far in institutionalizing the work of the Holy Spirit?
3. How do you respond to people who claim that the Holy Spirit has led them to do or say something? Do you think that the Spirit actually conveys truths or guidance to people today, for example, when they are making decisions during presidential elections?
4. How can we tell whether a group or an action is of God or of human design?

Chapter 9. I Believe in the Holy Catholic Church, the Communion of Saints

1. How important is it to you to belong to a specific branch of the Christian church?
2. How do you respond to critics of the church who say that there are too many hypocrites in it?
3. Should the various Christian churches try harder to engage in dialogue and work toward greater cooperation

with one another, or should each denomination try to gain more loyalty to its own tradition?

4. What do you think it means that the Apostles' Creed defines the "holy catholic church" as the "communion of saints"?

Chapter 10. I Believe in the Forgiveness of Sins

1. Do you believe in free will in the sense that we are able not to sin? Why or why not?

2. What difference does it make whether we think of sin primarily as personal and individual or primarily as unjust structures of society?

3. Do you think that the consciousness of sin has diminished in our culture? If so, why?

4. What does it mean for you to confess that Jesus "died for our sins"?

Chapter 11. I Believe in the Resurrection and the Life Everlasting

1. The psalmist prays, "So teach us to count our days that we may gain a wise heart" (Psalm 90:12). Is it good to dwell on the end of life, or will such thoughts ruin our enjoyment of life? What can we learn from the fact that we are mortal?

2. Someone has said, "Death must be distinguished from dying, with which it is often confused." That is, the fear of death can be more difficult to deal with than the actual experience of dying. Do you agree?

3. What biblical passages do you find comforting when thinking about the end of life?
4. Reflect on the faith of family members or close friends who died with confidence in the resurrection and life everlasting.
5. How can we envision a completely perfected existence, such as we hope for in "life everlasting"?

Index of Biblical References

Index of Topics